Cambridge E

Elements in Wor
edited I
Edgar W. Sc
University of Regensburg

INHERITANCE AND INNOVATION IN THE EVOLUTION OF RURAL AFRICAN AMERICAN ENGLISH

Guy Bailey
University of Texas Rio Grande Valley

Patricia Cukor-Avila
University of North Texas

Juan Salinas
University of Texas Rio Grande Valley

CAMBRIDGE
UNIVERSITY PRESS

Shaftesbury Road, Cambridge CB2 8EA, United Kingdom

One Liberty Plaza, 20th Floor, New York, NY 10006, USA

477 Williamstown Road, Port Melbourne, VIC 3207, Australia

314–321, 3rd Floor, Plot 3, Splendor Forum, Jasola District Centre,
New Delhi – 110025, India

103 Penang Road, #05–06/07, Visioncrest Commercial, Singapore 238467

Cambridge University Press is part of Cambridge University Press & Assessment,
a department of the University of Cambridge.

We share the University's mission to contribute to society through the pursuit of
education, learning and research at the highest international levels of excellence.

www.cambridge.org
Information on this title: www.cambridge.org/9781009087711

DOI: 10.1017/9781009083591

First published 2022

A catalogue record for this publication is available from the British Library.

ISBN 978-1-009-08771-1 Paperback
ISSN 2633-3309 (online)
ISSN 2633-3295 (print)

Inheritance and Innovation in the Evolution of Rural African American English

Elements in World Englishes

DOI: 10.1017/9781009083591
First published online: September 2022

Guy Bailey
University of Texas Rio Grande Valley

Patricia Cukor-Avila
University of North Texas

Juan Salinas
University of Texas Rio Grande Valley

Author for correspondence: Patricia Cukor-Avila, patricia.cukor-avila@unt.edu

Abstract: This Element uses data from the Springville Project to explore how the functions of the inherited forms invariant *be* (from English sources) and zero (from creolization) have transformed during the twentieth century. Originally just alternative present tense copula/auxiliary forms, both features developed into aspectual markers – invariant *be* to mark durativity/habituality and zero to mark nonstativity. The motivation for these innovations were both sociocultural and linguistic. The Great Migration and its consequences provided a demographic and sociocultural context within which linguistic innovations could develop and spread. The mismatch between form and function within the present tense copula/auxiliary system and the grammatical ambiguities that affected both invariant *be* and zero provided linguistic triggers for this reanalysis. When taken together, the evolution of these forms illustrates how restructured linguistic subsystems (and eventually new varieties) emerge out of the interplay between inheritance and innovation.

This Element also has a video abstract: www.cambridge.org/ ElementsinWorldEnglishes_Bailey

Keywords: African American English, zero copula, invariant habitual *be*, Great Migration, grammatical reanalysis

ISBNs: 9781009087711 (PB), 9781009083591 (OC)
ISSNs: 2633-3309 (online), 2633-3295 (print)

Contents

1 Introduction

At first glance, a monograph on African American English (AAE) might seem a bit unusual in a series on World Englishes, but, in fact, the development of AAE shares much in common with the development of other postcolonial varieties of English, especially when examined historically. Its synchronic distinctiveness clearly situates it apart from regional and ethnic varieties of American English, and its diachronic development can be situated within Schneider's Dynamic Model (Schneider 2003, 2007). The Dynamic Model provides a framework to account for the rise of postcolonial varieties of English (PCE) whose development stemmed from contact between English-speaking colonizers, the settler (STL) strand, and native or indigenous populations, the indigenous (IDG) strand (Schneider 2003, 2007). For Schneider, the degree of linguistic contact between these two strands results from a combination of social and political conditions, which ultimately drives the evolution of PCEs through a succession of five developmental stages – foundation, exonormative stabilization, nativization, endonormative stabilization, and differentiation (see Buschfeld et al. 2014; Schneider 2003, 2007 for a more detailed overview of each stage). The primary difference between AAE and other PCE varieties, of course, is that AAE did not arise from English being brought by settlers to another area through colonialization as a result of trade, exploitation, or settlement colonies. Rather, it developed in plantation colonies when enslaved Africans were forcibly brought to areas where English had already been implanted as a de facto national language (Schneider 2003, 2007). The social and linguistic contact that Schneider outlines for people living in plantation colonies in the Caribbean bears a strong resemblance to what occurred in plantation colonies across the Southern United States from the Atlantic Coast to Central Texas. In both circumstances, the enslaved populations were multilingual, and in order "to fulfill their communicative needs as human beings, they were therefore forced to adjust to the new linguistic environment as rapidly and as effectively as possible under the circumstances" (Schneider 2007: 62). Schneider indicates that creolization then played a central role in the development of these PCEs as they developed from extensive contact-induced restructuring or "structural nativization" that occurred in the plantation societies (Schneider 2007: 60–63).[1] While the precise status of early AAE is still a matter of considerable debate (see, for example, the papers by

---

[1] Here we follow Holm (2004) and view creolization as a sociolinguistic process. In what follows, we are not implying that AAE was ever a "fully restructured language" in the same way that the Caribbean creoles that developed in plantation colonies are. Rather, we suggest that it went through many of the same sociolinguistic processes.

Mufwene, Rickford, Schneider, Van Herk, and Winford in Lanehart 2015; Poplack 2000; Poplack and Tagliamonte 2001; Rickford 2006; and Spears 2008), there is a widespread belief that it underwent at least some of the kind of contact-induced restructuring that characterizes not only the creole languages that emerged in the Caribbean but also Gullah, which emerged along the South Carolina–Georgia Coast.

In the United States, the indigenous languages both of Africans who were brought over during the initial phases of the slave trade and also of later arrivals from Africa and the Caribbean disappeared over time. However, the interactions of those languages with the English spoken by the White settler population (and by native-born enslaved people during subsequent phases of the slave trade) gave rise to a distinctive variety that has developed independently from varieties spoken by other groups, though certainly in interaction with those varieties, and has served as a marker of group solidarity throughout African American history. It is this distinctiveness of historical development, in concert with the variety's enormous cultural uniqueness and significance, that leads many scholars to refer to it as African American Language (AAL) rather than African American English. Because of our focus on the workings of innovation on linguistic antecedents, we use the term African American English, which more accurately reflects the dual linguistic heritage of AAE, but in a work focused on cultural contexts and contemporary uses, AAL might well be the more appropriate term.

The most frequently analyzed subsystem of AAE, present tense copula/ auxiliary *be*, is in many ways a microcosm of the evolution of AAE. As we show, the forms used to express present tense copula/auxiliary *be* in AAE reflect the dual heritage of the variety, but inheritance cannot in and of itself explain the distribution and function of present-day AAE copula/auxiliary forms. While it is quite likely that the AAE copula/auxiliary has evolved continuously from the time the first enslaved Africans were brought to the English colonies along the Eastern Seaboard, the paucity of evidence that exists before the twentieth century makes it difficult to do a detailed linguistic analysis of the early stages of that evolution. Data collected from interviews with former slaves in the 1930s and in the HOODOO transcripts, however, provides earlier benchmarks against which contemporary linguistic evidence can be compared (see Bailey, Maynor, and Cukor-Avila 1991; Ewers 1996; Kautzsch 2002, and Schneider 1989); data collected since the 1980s allows for a detailed analysis of developments in AAE over the course of the twentieth century. The synchronic approach to language change, first articulated by Weinreich, Labov, and Herzog (1968) and later amplified by many others, provides a mechanism for taking full advantage of this data. This Element uses the synchronic approach to language change in analyzing data from one of the largest corpora of twentieth-century AAE to show how two iconic, inherited forms of present tense copula/auxiliary *be*, zero copula and invariant *be*, were transformed over the course of the twentieth century, taking on new functions and meanings that reshaped the dynamics of the entire present tense copula/auxiliary system in both obvious and not-so-obvious ways. In doing so, the Element illustrates more generally how the interaction of inheritance with innovation can shape emerging varieties.

The fact that the earlier AAE present tense copula/auxiliary not only included the three forms present in almost all English varieties, *am*, *is*, and *are*, but also included zero and invariant *be*, made AAE distinctive, and it also created a mismatch between form and function in the copula/auxiliary system. In English, of course, the person/number of the subject governs the distribution of *am*, *is*, and *are*, although in some varieties *is* occurs in the plural as well.[2] Both this person/number system and also the forms *am*, *is*, and *are* comprise part of AAE's English inheritance. The form of invariant *be* is also an English inheritance, but it had lost its distinctive function by the time it was absorbed into AAE (see Bailey 1989 for a discussion of the evolution of invariant *be* in earlier English). As a result, this inherited invariant *be* was simply an alternative form of *are* and to a lesser extent *am* and *is*: it had no function or meaning that distinguished it from any other copula/auxiliary form.

While zero also lacked a distinctive function in earlier AAE, simply alternating with *is* and *are*, it clearly was not inherited from English, although the term *copula deletion*, which is often used for zero copula/auxiliary, implies that it is. That term comes from the argument that zero is the result of a deletion process in AAE that is simply an extension of the copula/auxiliary contraction of *is* and *are* that occurs in most varieties of English (Labov 1969). The implication here is that zero was not inherited from any source external to AAE but rather simply derives from the operations of this phonological process. As we show in Section 4, though, this deletion process cannot adequately explain zero – in fact, it does not account for more than 20 percent of the zeros in our data. The source of zero thus must lie elsewhere. The best evidence that the source of zero is not English lies in the factor that is most important in promoting its occurrence in AAE. In English, it is always the subject that determines the form of the verb. However, as a number of linguists have shown (see Blake 1997 and Rickford 1998 for a list of many of them, as well as excellent summaries of the literature on zero copula), the occurrence of zero in AAE is more heavily

---

[2] Even when *is* occurs as a plural in various dialects of English, it is still the subject that governs the form of the verb, although in this case it is the subject type (personal pronoun, noun phrase, or existential) rather than the person/number of the subject (see Bailey, Maynor, and Cukor-Avila 1989).

influenced by the following predicate than the preceding subject. Although the debate over the precise non-English source of zero has not been completely resolved (cf. Baugh 1980; McWhorter 1998; Mufwene 1996a, 1996b, 2015; Rickford 1998, 2015; Winford 1997, 1998, 2015), there can be little doubt but that the source is not English.

The presence of two copula/auxiliary forms without distinct functions, inherited from different sources, provides the starting point for a century of grammatical developments that reshaped one of the basic subsystems of AAE grammar.[3] Documenting these developments and exploring the linguistic conditions that motivated them and the social contexts in which they occurred is the focus of this Element.

2 An Approach to Analyzing the AAE Copula/Auxiliary System

The data for our examination of the evolution of the present tense copula/ auxiliary system in AAE comes from the Springville Project, one of the longest-running field studies in linguistics. After doing exploratory fieldwork in 1986–7, we began the Springville Project in the summer of 1988 and it is still ongoing.[4] As a result, the project provides (as of 2021) a thirty-three-year real time window on linguistic developments in the rural community of Springville; with informants born as early as 1893 and as late as 2002, it provides an apparent time perspective of more than a century. When combined with other mechanically recorded evidence from the same area (including several recordings made before World War II with former slaves as part of a Works Progress Administration (WPA) project that collected slave narratives), the real time window expands to more than three-quarters of a century and the apparent time window to more than a century and a half.[5]

2.1 Springville as a Research Site

Springville was chosen as a research site because it was typical of the kind of community in which more than half the population of the Lower South lived

---

[3] For good structural descriptions of AAE, see Green (1998, 2011).

[4] Springville is a pseudonym for the community. Some of the results of the exploratory fieldwork are published in Bailey (1993), Bailey and Maynor (1989), and Bailey, Maynor, and Cukor-Avila (1989). Some of the results of the fieldwork from 1988 onward are published in Cukor-Avila's (1995) dissertation and a large number of our articles that are referred to throughout this Element.

[5] Another promising database for longitudinal research on AAE is the Corpus of Regional African American Language (CORAAL) (Kendall and Farrington 2021), a publicly accessible online resource that contains downloadable sound files of recordings with African Americans from various regions of the United States with corresponding time-aligned word-for-word transcriptions and metadata.

between 1880 and 1940.[6] As late as 1910, more than 75 percent of African Americans in the United States lived in Southern rural communities like Springville. What is most important about Springville, then, is that it was *not* unique: it could have been one of a thousand similar communities around the South. In fact, the only thing atypical about Springville is that the village persisted as long as it did, something due almost entirely to the tenacity of the owners of the general store that stood at the center of this rural community.[7]

Rural communities (i.e., with populations of fewer than 2,500) organized around general stores were central to the system of farm tenancy that lay at the heart of the economic and social structure of the Lower South between 1880 and World War II.[8] Both these communities and the stores they were built around were largely a post–Civil War development (Ayers 1992). Ayers notes that during the last decades of the nineteenth century, more than 150,000 stores opened in the South, and most rural communities in the region were served by only one or two stores. Those stores often served as post offices; as middlemen between bankers and tenant farmers in the credit-based crop lien system that dominated the cotton South; and as central gathering places and loci of social and linguistic interaction in rural communities. As in Springville, the store owners often owned the land that tenants "rented" through crop liens. Stores were also the primary places where African Americans and Whites interacted publicly since schools and churches, the other two institutions in most rural communities, were segregated by law and custom.

Springville was one of those villages, organized around a general store, that emerged during the late nineteenth century, and the choice of Springville as a research site was tied to its place in the sociohistorical context outlined here. Located in some of the most fertile land in Texas, the Springville area was first settled by Anglos in the late 1830s and 1840s as cotton reached its natural western boundary. By 1860, most of the "Bottoms" (the prime cotton land between two rivers in the area) had been cleared by slaves, and many of the

---

[6] More than half the population of the South lived in rural areas (communities of less than 2,500 people) until after World War II. For a discussion of the urbanization of the South and its linguistic consequences, see Bailey et al. (1996), Tillery and Bailey (2003), and Tillery, Bailey, and Wikle (2004).

[7] The store closed in 2004, shortly after the owner's death. The post office, which was situated in the rear of the store, remained in operation for another decade until it was closed by the federal government.

[8] For a discussion of general stores and their role in the South, see Ayers (1992) and Bailey (1997). The classic study of the system of farm tenancy is Agee and Evans' *Let Us Now Praise Famous Men*, first published in 1941. The choice of Springville as a research site was inspired by Sprott, Alabama, a village that was one of the foci of Agee and Evans' study and a place where Bailey did fieldwork for the Pederson et al. (1981) *Linguistic Atlas of the Gulf States* in 1976. Like Springville, Sprott persisted throughout most of the twentieth century; the post office in the Sprott store closed in 1993.

families whose ownership of the lands would extend into the twenty-first century had established plantations. Both the size and character of these plantations were much like those elsewhere in the interior Lower South (e.g., the Alabama Black Belt and Mississippi Delta). Enslaved African Americans comprised a large majority of the population in the Bottoms.

As in other parts of the plantation South, after the Civil War, Springville area plantations reorganized to implement farm tenancy. One of the prominent planters established a general store in the area during the late 1860s, and, by the 1880s, a post office had been established at the store as well. Between 1880 and 1895, the village of Springville grew up rapidly around the store. By 1880, an African American church had been built (and has remained in continual operation since), and, in 1891, a rail line connecting Springville to the largest town in the county was completed, with the store serving as the depot. By 1895, the village included several other businesses, two churches, a school, and a population of 550. As an increasingly greater proportion of the land in the area was put into cotton production after 1880, former slaves were insufficient to supply the number of tenant farmers needed in the Bottoms. To supplement the African American tenants, planters began recruiting Whites from nearby areas, Mexican Americans from south Texas, Mexicans from Mexico, and Italians directly from Italy. (Descendants of all these groups remained in the Springville area throughout the twentieth century and are among those interviewed for the Springville Project). In addition, between 1880 and 1930, many of the Whites who owned small farms in the area lost them and became tenants too. By 1930, more than 75 percent of the farmers in the county in which Springville is located were tenants, with the vast majority of the land (especially in the Bottoms) owned by a few landowners. In spite of the growth of the White and Mexican American populations during the late nineteenth and early twentieth centuries, however, African Americans remained a majority into the twenty-first century.

After World War II, landowners rapidly mechanized their cotton production. Mechanization, of course, eliminated the need for tenants, and, by the early 1960s, the rural population of the Bottoms was less than half what it had been in 1940 as both African Americans and others moved to urban areas in search of work. Changes in the school-aged population (pre-kindergarten through grade 8) in the Springville Independent School District (ISD), which was formed in 1925, illustrate the magnitude of the exodus.[9] In 1925, more than 500 area children were enrolled in the two schools (one Black and one White)

---

[9] The scope of the Springville ISD, of course, extends beyond the boundaries of the village of Springville itself; it includes roughly the surrounding rural areas that the general store traditionally serviced.

that comprised the district; 63 years later only 58 students attended the consolidated school.[10]

In spite of the exodus from the village, the store owner and his descendants, unlike most store owners in the South, maintained their residence in Springville and continued to run the general store/post office. After the 1960s, the population stabilized at 150–170, and the community preserved a spatial and social organization through the end of twentieth century that was much like the one that had emerged during its post–Civil War development. The general store remained the focal point of the community and served as a central gathering place for Springville residents of all ages and races and a primary site of mutual linguistic interaction, even during the time that institutions such as churches and schools were segregated.

The history of Springville after the mid-1990s is unique in one way, though. While the community itself has continued to decline slightly in population and both the store and the post office located in the building that housed the store closed in 2004 and 2014, respectively, enrollment in the Springville School increased dramatically from a low of 42 students in 1989–90 to 273 students in 1999–2000, then to 615 in 2020–21. This increase was due not to any changes in the Springville community itself, but rather to the decision by the Springville Independent School District Board to admit students from outside the district. Because the Springville School was considered safer and of higher quality than the schools in nearby larger towns, many parents in those communities chose to have their children attend school in Springville. By the early 2000s, enrollment had grown enough so that the district decided to add grades 9–12 to the existing school, which had previously included only grades pre-kindergarten through 8. As we point out, the dramatic increase in the Springville School enrollment has led to equally dramatic changes in the demographic makeup of the school; this, in turn, has had some important linguistic consequences for younger Springville residents.

In spite of this unique development, Springville was quite typical of the kind of community where most African Americans lived during the first half of the twentieth century, and its subsequent history through the mid-1990s, characterized by outmigration and population loss, was typical as well. Because of their centrality to the economic and social structure of the Lower South before World War II, understanding communities like Springville is crucial to an understanding of the evolution of AAE in the South during the late nineteenth and the twentieth centuries. Springville, then, provides an ideal locale for understanding

---

[10] The more recent history of the school is quite interesting and may well have been the primary factor in the spread of quotative *be like* into the community. See Cukor-Avila (2012) for both a discussion of the later history of the school and of the spread of quotative *be like*.

the linguistic evolution of AAE in the kind of community in which most African Americans lived prior to World War II. It has also been an excellent place for doing the kind of fieldwork necessary to develop an adequate database for analyzing this evolution.

2.2 The Springville Corpus

The sample of residents interviewed in Springville mirrors the historical population of the village, which has always been about two-thirds African American, with Anglos and Mexican Americans comprising the remainder. The sample currently includes 103 people (67 Blacks, 24 Anglos, and 12 Mexican Americans). It also includes the full age spectrum of community residents during the time of the fieldwork, with the oldest participant born in 1893 and the youngest in 2002. As pointed out in Section 2.1, this provides an apparent time perspective on Springville of more than a century, while the longitudinal focus of the fieldwork provides a real time perspective of more than thirty years. Finally, the sample reflects the structure of the Springville community in at least two other ways. First, it includes fewer males than females born after World War II since males born after the war tended to leave the community as soon as they reached their late teen years. Females often left too, but they returned more frequently than males, either on a permanent or periodic basis, when they had children or as they needed to care for their elders. Second, Springville was a remarkably homogeneous community in terms of social factors such as education and social class. Most residents left high school before graduation, and only one went on to college. Our sample does include this resident, but it otherwise reflects the homogeneity of the community.

In addition to providing a sample that reflects the linguistic development of a community that was typical of the Cotton South, where most African Americans lived during the last quarter of the nineteenth and first half of the twentieth centuries, the Springville fieldwork had two additional priorities. First, it attempted to address the methodological problem of the observer's paradox, something that Labov (1966) first articulated and that many sociolinguists believe significantly affects the results of linguistic fieldwork, especially in African American communities. Second, it created a panel survey within the larger sample to address possible issues of age-grading that need to be resolved in using the apparent time construct to explore language change. To address the observer's paradox, the Springville fieldwork routinely made use of group interviews and site studies with both children and adults. These interview contexts created situations in which interlocutors included other community members in addition to or in lieu of the fieldworkers. The fieldworkers also

Table 1 Distribution of finite present tense copula/auxiliary forms (total number of tokens in each environment) among African Americans in the Springville corpus (totals exclude *ain't* and tokens before sibilants).

	Am	*Is*	*Are*	**Zero**	*Be*
Positive statements	4,191	11,618	1,080	6,873	1,210
Negatives	420	515	120	196	88
Questions	16	1,461	330	1,327	14
TOTAL = 29,459	4,627	13,594	1,530	8,396	1,312

obtained multiple interviews with as many informants as possible to address the issues of familiarity that sometimes constrain conversation in fieldwork (see Cukor-Avila and Bailey [1995a, 2001] for a complete description of the field methods). To create a panel survey, nineteen of the African Americans in the sample, born between 1912 and 2002, were re-interviewed in as many years as possible after the initial baseline fieldwork was done in 1988/9 to form the panel (see Cukor-Avila and Bailey [2017] for a description of the panel survey).[11]

Cukor-Avila did word-for-word transcripts of each of the interviews. These transcripts create a corpus of more than 2,500,000 words of African American speech from the Springville community. The extensive database analyzed here comes from that corpus, and it includes very large numbers of relevant linguistic features, including almost 30,000 finite, present tense, copula/auxiliary forms (exclusive of *ain't* and 3rd singular tokens before sibilants).[12] Table 1 illustrates the size of the Springville corpus by summarizing the distribution of the copula/auxiliary forms in it by sentence type and realization (*am*, *is*, *are*, zero, and *be*). As it shows, the corpus includes close to 8,400 instances of zero copula/auxiliary and over 1,300 instances of invariant *be*, the two forms under analysis here.

---

[11] The panel survey thus includes almost 30 percent of the total number of African Americans interviewed. Both the length of time residents remained in the panel and the frequency with which they were interviewed depended to a large extent on their personal histories. Six of the nineteen panelists died during the thirty-plus year span of the project, and three who were born after the initial fieldwork began in 1988–9 were added as they became old enough for interviews. One of the informants moved out of the area and could not be contacted for interviews after 2002. Although the Springville panel survey suffers from the same issues of panel attrition that face all panel surveys, two-thirds of the panelists (twelve of nineteen) have remained as part of the panel throughout the duration of the project and were interviewed as recently as 2019. No additional fieldwork was done between 2019 and 2022 because of the COVID-19 pandemic.

[12] We have excluded *ain't* both from the database and from the discussion that follows. Because it has so many functions in African American English (AAE), we treat *ain't* as a single negating morpheme (see Bailey and Maynor 1985a). We have also excluded 3rd singular tokens before sibilants since in most cases it is impossible to determine whether or not -*s* is there.

The analysis of invariant *be* and zero in this Element includes most, but not all, of the forms in Table 1; the exclusions are described in Section 5.

2.3 Analysis of the Data

Until the mid-1960s, the operative assumption in the study of language change was that change could only be studied through its results: the observation of change as it was taking place was not possible (see Hockett 1958). The articulation of a synchronic approach to language change in the work of Labov (1963, 1966, 1972a, 1994, 2001, 2010), however, provided linguists with a vehicle for studying change as it was occurring; for examining the mechanisms by which linguistic changes take place; and for exploring the motivations for changes. The synchronic approach to language change grew out of two crucial insights: that linguistic change was intimately related to linguistic variation and that variation and change could be tracked as they were taking place in the speech of different generations of adults (i.e., in *apparent time*). The Springville Project was designed in part to take advantage of these insights and to use the methods that Labov and others devised for the synchronic approach to language change.

The apparent time construct, of course, is a cornerstone of the synchronic approach (see Bailey et al. 1991; Cukor-Avila and Bailey 2013; Fruehwald 2017; Labov 1994; Tagliamonte and D'Arcy 2009). The basic assumption of apparent time is that the vernacular people learn in their adolescent and teenage years is, for the most part, the vernacular they use throughout their lives: the speech of each generation generally reflects the language as it existed at the time that generation learned it. Generational differences, when viewed in light of other characteristics of the synchronic distribution of features, thus become a surrogate for real time differences. Although the apparent time construct has been used successfully for more than half a century now, some researchers have questioned the assumption that the vernacular learned in the adolescent and teenage years generally remains the vernacular used throughout adulthood (see, for instance, Rickford and Price 2013; Sankoff 2018; Sankoff and Blondeau 2007). Two issues in particular are problematic for the assumption of vernacular maintenance: the possibility that some features are age-graded (i.e., individuals change in the use of those features during the course of their lifetimes even though the community as a whole does not change) (Wagner 2012), and the possibility of life-span change among individuals (i.e., "individual speakers change over their life spans in the direction of a change in progress in the rest of the community" [Sankoff 2005: 1011]).

An early comprehensive test of apparent time provided strong validation of the construct as an analytical tool (see Bailey, et al. 1991), and results in a later study "show overwhelming support for the apparent time model of investigating language change: most changes are incremented between generational cohorts, and have little intergenerational instability" (Fruehwald 2017: 24). However, assumptions regarding the maintenance of individual vernaculars have only recently begun to be tested.

The best mechanism for accurately assessing issues regarding vernacular maintenance is a panel survey – a survey in which informants are re-interviewed for the same variables over a period of years. The panel survey contained within the Springville Project includes a cross section of the population and thus allows for a comprehensive assessment of vernacular maintenance. Cukor-Avila and Bailey (2007), Cukor-Avila and Bailey (2013), and Tillery and Bailey (2003) demonstrate that the speech of individuals in the panel survey confirms the assumption of vernacular maintenance with two exceptions: durative/habitual *be* and quotative *be like*. In both cases, though, the changes in individual vernaculars support rather than contradict the results of apparent time analyses.

Although the emergence and spread of invariant *be* as a durative/habitual marker took place primarily during the second and third quarters of the twenti-eth century (see Section 3), among Springville residents born in the 1970s and 1980s, the feature is initially used at frequencies that are more like those of their grandparents than their parents. However, as these adolescents go to a nearby urban area to attend high school, their frequencies increase to match and even exceed those of the previous generation. Cukor-Avila and Bailey (2007, 2011) argue that this is an instance of "diffusional age-grading" and is actually part of the mechanism that leads to the spread of durative/habitual *be*. As Labov (2007) has noted, age-grading of this sort is necessary for linguistic changes to expand, and it is entirely compatible with the apparent time construct.

As quotative *be like* began to diffuse into Springville, it showed evidence both of age-grading, as residents born after the mid-1970s began to acquire the form, and of life-span changes, as two older panelists began to use the form occasionally. With both the diffusional age-grading and life-span changes, the shifts in individual vernaculars are not only in the direction of the linguistic innovation occurring in the community (Labov 2007), but, more important, are part of the mechanism for the spread of *be like*. They do not affect the patterns and trajectories of change suggested by the apparent time data. While the shifts in individual vernaculars provide insight into some of the mechanisms that amplify the spread of these innovations, the apparent time data from Springville provides the clearest picture of the evolution of durative/habitual *be* and zero copula and of their situation within larger demographic and historical forces that provided the context for their evolution. Thus, apparent time remains the focus of this Element.[13]

As Labov (1969: 728) has noted, the study of variation, which is foundational to the synchronic approach to language change, "is necessarily quantitative, and quantitative analysis necessarily involves counting." The Springville corpus includes an extremely large number of instances of zero and invariant *be* and thus allows for substantial counting, and for a wide range of statistical approaches as well. Statistical analysis is particularly important in our investigation of zero since we are proposing a new model for this feature – and, in turn, challenging one that has been widely accepted for half a century and that is used in almost all of the prior work on the feature. To validate our approach and to show that it provides a better explanation of the evidence, our investigation of zero utilizes the binary logistic regression program in SPSS to analyze the quantitative data. Binary logistic regression estimates the influence of one or several predictor variables on a dichotomous dependent variable. All predictor variables (e.g., subject type and predicate type) are categorical variables and are used to assess both the statistical significance and the effect size (Nagelkerke's R^2) for the overall model. The R^2 provides an indication of the amount of variance explained by a group of predictor variables and an indication of the goodness of fit between the data and the model, with higher R^2s generally reflecting a good fit and lower ones a poorer fit. As Freedman points out, however, in the social sciences low R^2s are not infrequent ("in fields like political science and sociology, $R^2 < 1/10$ is commonplace" [Freedman 2009: 52]). The R^2s in this investigation are much higher than that, though, and demonstrate an excellent fit between the data and the model we propose.

As the results in the following sections show, the corpus and the analytical approach outlined here provide significant insight into the evolution of the two most iconic features of the AAE present tense copula/auxiliary system, invariant *be* and zero. In doing so, they demonstrate how the interplay between inheritance and innovation can transform the grammar of a linguistic subsystem.

---

[13] Although the Springville corpus is what Fruehwald calls a "multistage corpus" and offers the possibility of exploring temporal effects along several dimensions (e.g., year of birth of informants, age of the informant at the time of various interviews, and years in which various interviews were done), year of birth, the focus of the apparent time construct, provides the clearest picture of the temporal development of the features under investigation in this Element as well as the features investigated in Fruehwald's study. Variation by age of the informant at the time of the interview (as seen in analyses of the panel survey data) is revealing only insofar as it highlights mechanisms that amplify the spread of innovations, and the year of the interview has no independent explanatory value for either variable. Using tensor product smooths to analyze the three dimensions simultaneously (see Fruehwald 2017) is complicated by differences in the number of tokens per interview and in various years that interviews were done (see Cukor-Avila and Bailey [2017] for a discussion of the effects of varying N sizes). Note also that Fruehwald's (2017) use of the tensor product smooths shows strong support for the use of apparent time as an analytical tool.

3 Invariant *be*

The use of an uninflected *be* where other varieties of English have the copula/ auxiliary forms *are*, *am*, and *is* (as in examples 1 to 3) is one of the most distinctive features of twentieth-century AAE.[14]

1. You know only time *we really be busy* is on Saturday's. [f/1961/1989][15]
2. You know when I'm at Wal-Mart an' *I be outside* an' it's hot I'll go in there an' play video. [f/1979/1988]
3. *She be up and down the road* all day long an' I tol' her if she don' mind then I'm not gonna let her go. [f/1961/1992]

A large body of research on this uninflected or invariant *be* has shown clearly that the form is a durative/habitual marker in contemporary AAE and that its occurrence is quite widespread (see, for example, Bailey and Maynor 1987, 1989; Dayton 1996; Fasold 1972; Labov et al.1968; Rickford 1992; Wolfram 1969, 1974, and Wolfram and Thomas 2008). Although some of the early research on AAE hypothesized that the feature emerged through a restructuring of an earlier creole form such as *de* (see Stewart 1967, 1968), since the work of Bailey and Maynor (1987) most linguists have recognized that invariant *be* in contemporary AAE actually represents the reanalysis of an earlier English form and is a fairly recent development (see Wolfram and Thomas 2008, for example). As we demonstrate in the following section, the development of invariant *be* as a durative/habitual marker in AAE was a complicated process that resulted from the interplay of innovation and inheritance, and it illustrates the kind of restructuring that leads to the emergence of distinctive varieties.

3.1 Invariant *be* in Earlier English and in Earlier AAE

An invariant *be* used where many contemporary varieties have *are* has a long history in English. In Middle English, *be*, *ben*, and *been* were the most common plural forms in the present tense of *be*, with *are(n)* restricted largely to dialects of the North and parts of the Midland (Moore and Marckwardt 1969). Further, *be/ben/been* were the dominant plural forms in the written documents from which standard written English developed (e.g., in Chaucer and the writings of

---

[14] While zero is well-documented in earlier written documents and in the earliest scholarly work on AAE (Harrison 1884), there are not many instances of invariant *be* in those documents, and the form is not mentioned by Harrison.

[15] All the examples in this Element come from the Springville corpus. The speaker's gender, year of birth, and the date of the recording follow each example.

the Chancery clerks). During the fifteenth century, *are* gradually began to spread south and west at the expense of *be*, but even at the end of the fifteenth century *be* seems to have been used much more often than *are*. For example, "in Hanham's edition of the Cely letters, written between 1472 and 1488, *be* accounts for 58% of the plural tokens, with *are* accounting for only 13% (*ben*, *beth*, and *is* make up the remainder")" (Bailey 1989: 160).

Starting around 1530 and continuing over the next two centuries, the early grammars of English and the comparative grammars of English and other languages that began to appear document the continued spread of *are* and the gradual relegation of *be* to a dialect form that occurred largely in the south and west of England. They show that, by the middle of the eighteenth century, *be* had come to be considered archaic in standard English.[16] Bailey (1989) summarizes this evidence:

> The early grammars of Du Wes (1532) and Thomas (1550) give only *be* as the plural form of *to be*, while later sixteenth-century grammarians list *be* and *are* as alternative forms. It is not until Le Mayre's *The Dutch School-Master*, published in 1606, that any grammar gives *are* only as a plural, but after 1550 no grammarian gives only *be*, although in the seventeenth century most grammars still list *are* and *be* as alternative forms. While some grammarians, including Bishop Lowth, continued to list *are* and *be* as alternative forms as late as the middle of the eighteenth century, the use of *be* was becoming archaic, as Lowth himself indicates (Bailey 1989: 161).

When English was brought to what is now the United States in the seventeenth century, then, *be* was still used as a plural form but was becoming archaic. It continued to flourish in some regional dialects of England that were brought across the Atlantic, however. Africans transported to the British colonies would have encountered this fluid linguistic situation, with *be* occurring alongside *are* at least to some extent in many places. Over the next two centuries, the use of invariant *be* continued to diminish in American as well as in British English, but as late as the early twentieth century it could be found occasionally in White as well as Black speech in the American South, especially in rural areas. Using data from Pederson's (1981) *Linguistic Atlas of the Gulf States*, Bailey and Bassett (1986) document the occasional use of the form in eastern Louisiana in the speech of both African Americans and Whites born in the last decades of the nineteenth century and first two decades of the twentieth, though they find it is less frequent in White speech. Based on their fieldwork in Texas and Mississippi, Bailey and Maynor (1985a, 1985b) also document it in similar

---

[16] Those grammars also document *be* as a present subjunctive form in all person and numbers. The influence of this use of invariant *be* on later developments is not clear but is probably worth exploring.

populations in those states, although again it is rare among Whites and not especially frequent among African Americans. While *be* occurs most often in the plural or second singular in both studies, it does occur in 1st person singular and, less often, in 3rd singular as well. More important, invariant *be* at this point had no special function: it was simply an alternative form for *are* and less frequently for *am* and *is*.

Invariant *be*, then, clearly occurred as an alternative for *are* (and to a lesser extent for *am* and *is*) in the speech of African Americans in the South at the end of the nineteenth and beginning of the twentieth century, but the situation was actually more complex than this. That complexity, we believe, played a significant role in the evolution of invariant *be* into a durative/habitual marker in AAE over the course of the twentieth century. The complicating factor lies in the fact that there was a second type of invariant *be* in AAE (and in some older Southern White varieties) during the late nineteenth and early twentieth centuries. While this second type of invariant *be* was identical in form to the first, the two types were quite different structurally and functionally. This second type of invariant *be* was actually an infinitival rather than a finite form, and it resulted from the deletion of a preceding *will* or *would*, as in examples 4 and 5:

4. But *it be so hot*. Because we used to chop from sun to sun an' that was tough. [m/1932/1988]
5. Nuh uh it'll make you drowsy an' *you be sleepy*. [f/1961/1997]

To distinguish the invariant *be* that is an alternative for *are*, *am*, and *is* from the one derived from the deletion of *will/would*, some linguists refer to the former as *be₂*. To avoid confusion, we will do so as well. Fasold (1972) has a detailed discussion of the differences between the two types of invariant *be* and lays out a set of criteria for distinguishing between them (for example, *be* derived from *will/would* deletion is negated by *won't/wouldn't*, while be_2 is negated by *don't*).[17] It is important to note, however, that the distinction between these two types of invariant *be* is not always clear in actual usage, as examples 6 and 7 show. As we suggest in Section 5, the ambiguity that sometimes occurs, along with the formal similarity between be_2 and the invariant *be* derived from *will/would* deletion, may well have been factors in the reanalysis of be_2 that we describe.

6. She useta take Tina an' them down there, an' go drop Tina. An' Tina, drop her off an' she'll be cryin'. *I be like*, "What's wrong?" "I wanna go back up

---

[17] Fasold's (1972) analysis of the various kinds of invariant *be* provides the foundation for all subsequent work on the subject, including that in this Element. While our data suggests differences with his analysis on a few points, his overall analysis remains quite sound.

there with Mama. I don' wanna stay down here in this house. I don't like it down here." [f/1982/1999]

7. 'Cause they told me if I didn't bring the trailer, you know, *I be havin' them puttin'* that up there in vain. I said, "No the trailer's comin', it's comin'."
[f/1931/2009]

Although *be$_2$* forms have been documented occasionally in AAE since its beginnings, as Bailey and Maynor (1985a, 1987, 1989) demonstrate, in nineteenth- and early twentieth-century varieties, infinitival invariant *be* (the one derived from *will/would* deletion as in examples 4 and 5) actually occurred much more often than *be$_2$*; neither of these, however, was exactly the same as the durative/habitual *be* described in research on twentieth-century AAE. Over the course of the twentieth century, infinitival invariant *be* began to recede while *be$_2$* expanded rapidly and took on new functions and distributions. It is this *be$_2$*, with its new functions and distributions, that research on twentieth-century AAE describes, and it is largely a development of the last three-quarters of that century.[18] Data from Springville clearly documents the expansion and reanalysis of *be$_2$*.

3.2 The Development of Invariant *be* in Twentieth-Century AAE

The Springville data includes 1,344 tokens of the various types of invariant *be*: 1,169 tokens of *be$_2$*, 132 tokens of *be* derived from *will/would* deletion, 34 ambiguous forms (tokens that could be either *be$_2$* or the result of *will/would* deletion), and 9 forms that seem to be simple past tense forms as in examples 8 and 9:

8. Cause I worked at practically every farm down in here. An' really, I mean, but more work on the R. farm thirty years. *Thirty years I be over there.* Thirty years. I been here thirty-three years. [f/1912/1996]

9. Oh I woke up a many a night with a toothache an' had to have 'em pulled the nex' day. An' then my mother, in those days my mother had somethin' called bullet moles an' she took in on that tooth an' she'd get it out there *if you didn' be careful*. [f/1912/1988]

As this list suggests, the term invariant *be* encompasses a range of forms. These forms are not always clearly distinguished from each other in the literature, and they are not always easily distinguishable from each other in actual usage, as the ambiguous forms cited in examples 6 and 7 suggest. While all these types persist throughout the twentieth century, an examination of *be$_2$* and infinitival

---

[18] See Bailey and Bassett (1986), Bailey and Maynor (1985a, 1987), and Bailey (2007) for more details on invariant *be* and its evolution as a durative/habitual marker.

invariant *be* in apparent time clearly shows that, over the course of the century, (1) *be₂* expanded dramatically at the expense of invariant *be* derived from *will/would* deletion until the latter became a relatively rare form and (2) *be₂* became highly focused and developed a specific function, essentially eliminating all nondurative/nonhabitual uses. By the last forty years of the century, *be₂* had become the distinctive durative/habitual *be* that Fasold (1972), Labov (1972b), Labov et al. (1968), Wolfram (1969), and Wolfram and Thomas (2008), among others, identified and described in mid and late twentieth-century AAE. (We are excluding the past tense uses of invariant *be* from the discussion here, since they account for less than 1 percent of the total invariant *be* corpus. Although they occur among all age groups, it is not clear that they are not mistakes).

This reanalysis of invariant *be* seems to have taken place in three overlapping stages. The first stage involved the expansion of invariant *be₂* at the expense of *be* derived from *will/would* deletion. As Figure 1 shows, in the mechanically recorded data from former slaves, several of whom lived near the Springville area (see Bailey, Maynor, and Cukor-Avila 1991), invariant *be* derived from *will/would* deletion accounted for more than three-quarters of the tokens in the total invariant *be* corpus; it still comprised more than half of the invariant *be* tokens for Springville residents born in first two decades of the twentieth century. Figure 1 also shows the rapid expansion of *be₂* as a proportion of all invariant *be* tokens among the three younger age groups. Among Springville residents born between 1921 and 1944, *be₂* accounted for more than 80 percent of the invariant *be* tokens, and among those born between 1945 and 1965, it

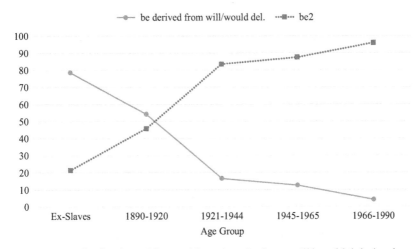

Figure 1 Distribution of *be₂* and invariant *be* from *will/would* deletion in apparent time. (Totals exclude ambiguous and past tense tokens).

comprised almost 90 percent. Among those born after 1966, invariant *be*
derived from *will/would* deletion represented less than 5 percent of the invariant
be tokens in the data, while *be₂* accounted for just over 95 percent. Although we
defer the discussion of what triggered the change in the distribution of the two
different types of invariant *be* (one derived from *will/would* deletion and one
serving as an alternative copula/auxiliary form) to Section 5, other aspects of its
distribution suggest that the expansion of *be₂* at the expense of infinitival
invariant *be* is the first stage in a reanalysis of the form (see Bailey and
Maynor 1987).

The second stage of the reanalysis involved the development of restrictions
on the uses of *be₂* as it expanded. In nineteenth-century varieties of AAE, *be₂*
was used with the same range of meanings that *am, is,* and *are* have, with no
particular preference for durative/habitual contexts (see Bailey and Bassett
1986 for documentation of this). As Figure 2 shows, none of the tokens of *be₂*
used for *am, is,* and *are* by former slaves was in a durative or habitual context.
Among Springville residents born in the first two decades of the twentieth
century, however, the use of *be₂* in durative/habitual contexts increased dramatically and accounted for roughly three-quarters of the tokens. Among respondents born after 1921 the use of *be₂* in durative/habitual contexts continued to
expand, so that for residents born in the latter half of the twentieth century, *be₂*
almost always occurred in those contexts. The expansion of *be₂* as a durative/

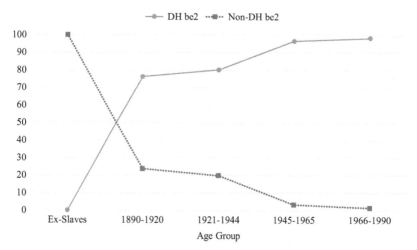

Figure 2 Distribution of durative habitual *be₂* and nondurative/nonhabitual *be₂*
in apparent time.

habitual form, of course, was matched by its decline in other contexts. As Figure 2 shows, among the youngest respondents, nondurative/nonhabitual uses accounted for less than 2 percent of the be_2 tokens.

Clearly, then, the occurrence of be_2 increasingly correlated with durative/habitual contexts over the course of the twentieth century. As this happened, the uses both of invariant *be* derived from *will/would* deletion and also of non-durative/nonhabitual be_2 declined so rapidly that by the end of the century they were quite infrequent. A look at how all of the durative/habitual contexts within the present tense copula/auxiliary are marked in the Springville data suggests that this is more than simple correlation: it shows, rather, that over time, be_2 was reanalyzed so that it became a durative/habitual marker. Although there are not many tokens of be_2 in the data from former slaves, none of them was used in durative/habitual contexts, so those contexts were typically signaled through the occurrence of the appropriate adverbial. As Figure 3 shows, among the oldest Springville residents, less than half of the durative/habitual contexts in the present tense copula/auxiliary were marked by be_2. The majority of the dura-tive/habitual contexts involved an inflected form of *be* or zero co-occurring with an adverbial that signals either habituality or durativity, as in examples 10 to 12. Among the two age groups born after 1945, however, the number of durative

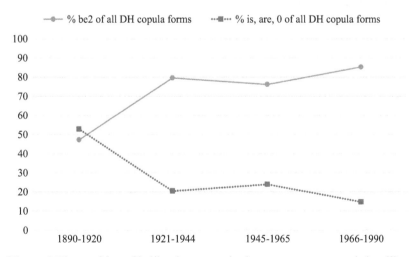

Figure 3 The marking of habitual contexts in the present tense copula/auxiliary in apparent time by be_2 versus *is, are, 0*. (Totals exclude 1st person singular).

/habitual contexts marked by *be* increased to between 76 percent and 85 percent respectively.

10. 'Cause uh, she had a operation two years ago in May an' they still give her trouble too. *She's always complainin'*. [f/1912/1988]
11. I come over here, *you're always here*. [m/1913/1988]
12. Boy *they always tryin'* to tease me. [m/1913/1989]

As the functional reanalysis of be_2 progressed during the twentieth century, a third stage in the reanalysis also occurred. As Figure 4 shows, syntactic restrictions followed closely behind the reanalysis of the meaning and function of be_2. None of the tokens of invariant *be* used by former slaves preceded *-ing* verbs, and among the oldest Springville residents, only a little more than 10 percent of the tokens did. Among the second oldest generation, however, the percentage of *be* before an *-ing* verb almost doubled, and among the two youngest generations, *be+v+ing* comprised over 60 percent of the tokens. Among Springville residents born after 1966, then, the grammatical reanalysis of be_2 seems to have gone to completion: what was once simply an occasional alternative copula/auxiliary form used in place of *am/is/are* became a durative/habitual marker in the present tense of *to be*, used primarily as an auxiliary before *-ing* verbs (as in example 13), to a lesser extent as a copula before locative and adjective forms (as in examples 14 and 15), and occasionally as a copula before NPs (example 16).

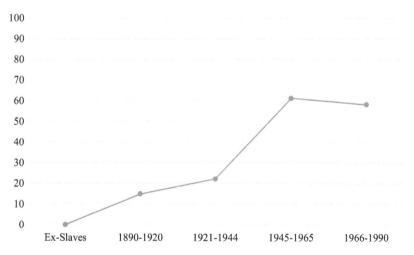

Figure 4 The percentage of *be+v+ing* out of all be_2 forms in apparent time.

13. 'Cause that's all them *young girls be wantin'* they nails done an' they hair. An' buy those little short dresses. [f/1961/1997]

14. An' like *they be up there* so long like some of the mangers they be like, "Yall still up here!" You know every time they pass by there, "Yall still up here?" [f/1982/2010]

15. I mean, you know, it's convenience an' I enjoy workin' for Miss Loretta. An' she's, she's nice. Uh, an' you know only time *we really be busy* is on Saturday's. So it's not a hard job. [f/1961/1989]

16. He an' his son work together pullin' tooth. *His wife be his secretary.* [f/1912/1988]

Note that the tokens used as auxiliaries (i.e., before v+*ing*, as in example 13) usually mark habituality, while those used as a copula (as in examples 14 to 16) often mark durativity.

This scenario for the development of durative/habitual *be* receives strong support from Ewers' (1996) analysis of invariant *be* in the HOODOO texts, a large set of which was collected between 1936 and 1940 (from informants born mostly in the late nineteenth and very early twentieth centuries) and a smaller set of which was collected in the 1970s from similar informants. The informants represented in the earlier HOODOO texts are thus similar to the oldest Springville informants (those born between 1890 and 1920), while those in the later texts are probably more like the Springville informants born between 1921 and 1944. The data for invariant *be* in the HOODOO texts is remarkably similar to that in Springville. In the early HOODOO texts, only 47 percent of the invariant *be* tokens carry habitual meaning, while in the later texts, 72.2 percent of them do. Further, in the early texts, just under 10 percent occur before a present participle; in the later texts, 15 percent of them do. The HOODOO texts, then, show the development both of the semantic and syntactic restrictions that were crucial in the evolution of durative/habitual *be* in Springville.

Just how fundamental durative/habitual *be* had become to the grammar of Springville AAE by the last decade of the twentieth century is demonstrated by the development of quotative *be like* in the speech of the youngest age group of residents. Quotative *be like* apparently entered Springville speech during the mid- to late-1990s, when the feature was most likely borrowed by children in the community as they attended school with large numbers of White and Hispanic children who came to the Springville school from nearby urban areas (see Cukor-Avila 2002, 2012 for a complete account of the emergence of quotative *be like* in the community). The data from these younger residents includes 187 *be like* quotatives. Of those 187, 86 comprise durative/habitual contexts, and of those 86, 73 (84.5 percent) are marked by be_2, as in examples 17 and 18. So fundamental is durative/habitual *be* in the grammar of the youngest Springville residents, then, that even borrowed features adapted this distinctive morphosyntactic structure. As a result, a feature that has emerged in the same form across the world (cf. Tagliamonte, D'Arcy, and Louro 2016) develops in unique ways in Springville, marked by be_2 when it occurs in durative/habitual contexts.

17. A lot of 'em, "Brandy you are the reason why I come in here." You know they, "Brandy you're my woman. I love you." You know all this type of stuff. So that's Kim Crazy. Girl she so crazy. *She be like*, "Brandy you're my woman an' I love you!" [f/1982/2010]
18. He, he, I guess he be tryin' to see if it somebody else be callin' to the house for me. *I be like*, "Matt I know it is you." [f/1982/2002]

At the beginning of the twentieth century, then, two types of invariant *be* forms existed in AAE in Springville, one an alternative form for *are* (and to a lesser extent *am* and *is*) and the other an infinitival form derived from the deletion of a preceding *will* or *would*. The latter occurred more frequently than the former. Over the course of the century, however, the former expanded rapidly, developing into a durative/habitual marker within the present tense copula/auxiliary system. As it did so, the occurrences of invariant *be* resulting from *will/would* deletion almost (but not entirely) disappeared, until they comprised less than 5 percent of the tokens of invariant *be* among the youngest age group in the corpus. Further, as be_2 became increasingly focused in durative/habitual contexts, nondurative/nonhabitual uses of the form also declined dramatically, from nearly a quarter of the tokens among the oldest age group to less than 2 percent among the youngest. An inherited form, in this case from English, was thus reanalyzed to create a unique, innovative morphosyntactic structure that became so fundamental to the grammar that even borrowed forms were adapted to it. In Section 5, we discuss some of the factors that led to the innovative use of this inherited form. In Section 4, we discuss changes in the use of another inherited feature of the AAE present tense copula/auxiliary system, zero. These developments are more subtle than the ones with invariant *be*; in fact, most research does not even recognize that these changes have taken place and simply treats zero as a stable feature. Nevertheless, as Section 4 demonstrates, the changes have occurred, and they are important in the overall restructuring of the AAE copula/auxiliary system.

4 Zero Copula/Auxiliary

Zero copula/auxiliary may be the most frequently analyzed feature in the vast body of research on AAE and perhaps in the entire field of quantitative sociolinguistics. In fact, Labov's early work on zero in AAE (Labov 1969, 1972b; Labov et al. 1968) was crucial in developing the approach to quantitative reasoning that still undergirds the discipline, and it also provided the foundation for almost all subsequent work on zero over the last sixty years. As we point out in Section 4.1, this foundational work also has important implications for our understanding of the historical development of both zero copula/auxiliary and also AAE more generally. A detailed examination of Labov's work and of those who follow will show how that work has shaped conclusions about zero and its history; our analysis of the Springville data will offer some alternative conclusions.

4.1 Labov's Approach to Zero Copula/Auxiliary

Based on his data from African Americans in New York City, Labov made several important observations about zero copula in AAE (Labov 1969, 1972b). He noted that:

- zero copula did not occur in past tense or in nonfinite structures;
- zero copula typically did not occur in 1st person singular;
- the occurrence of zero where other varieties have *are* quite likely stemmed from the same desulcalization processes that led to the absence of post-vocalic /r/ in AAE and hence was probably a separate process from the occurrence of zero where other varieties of English have *is*;
- zero copula did not occur in environments (e.g., clause finally, emphatically, and with invariant *be*) where contraction could not occur in other varieties of English: where contraction was prohibited in other varieties, zero was prohibited in his NYC data.

As a result of these observations, Labov constructed an envelope of variation for analyzing zero that excluded past, nonfinite, 1st singular present, and uncontractible forms (including invariant *be*), and he focused his analysis of zero copula on those contexts where other varieties of English have *is* since he believed zero for *are* to be the result of the same desulcalization process that led to the loss of postvocalic /r/ in AAE and not the result of the copula/auxiliary deletion process that affects *is*. As he narrowed the focus to *is* and related zero forms, Labov further excluded from the envelope of variation forms that precede a sibilant since the presence of a contracted /s/ is difficult to distinguish from zero in those environments. Finally, he suggested that forms following *it*, *that*, and *what* undergo an assibilation process that causes the final /t/ to be deleted, with the forms realized as *i's*, *tha's*, and *wha's* almost invariably. As a result, he excluded them from his analysis as well.[19] Essentially, then, Labov excluded from the envelope of variation for analyzing zero not only all environments where zero does not occur (or occurs infrequently), but also all environments where contraction cannot occur.

Based on the results generated through this envelope of variation, Labov then posited an explicit rule relationship between the copula/auxiliary contraction that occurs in all varieties of English and zero, which is primarily an AAE feature: zero is the result of a deletion process (a phonological process) that operates on the output of copula/auxiliary contraction. He called this process "copula deletion." Labov thus provided an elegant and sophisticated account of zero copula/auxiliary that explained one of the most complicated stereotypes of AAE and also accounted for the many parallels to the process of contraction that is universal in English. Finally, given the relationship between contraction and deletion, Labov developed a formula for calculating rates of deletion in a corpus: deleted forms represent a percentage of contracted plus deleted forms (D/C+D).

Both the envelope of variation and the analytical approach that Labov developed are still used in most research on zero with a couple of exceptions. First, Wolfram (1974) argued that, based on similarities in the factors that influence their occurrence, zero forms that appear where other varieties have *are* should in fact be included along with third singular forms in the envelope of variation for zero copula.[20] As a result of Wolfram's analysis, the inclusion of 3rd and 1st person plural and 2nd person forms alongside 3rd singular forms is now the norm for the analysis of zero.[21] Second, researchers have proposed an alternative mechanism for calculating copula deletion – what has become known as *straight deletion* (as opposed to *Labov deletion*). Straight deletion computes deleted forms as a percentage of full, contracted, and deleted forms (D/F+C+D) rather than as a percentage of contracted and deleted forms, as Labov had done (see Blake 1997; Rickford 1998; and Rickford et al. 1992 for extensive discussions of these issues, of the envelope of variation more

---

[19] See Bailey and Maynor (1987) for further discussion of Labov's analysis of *i's*, *tha's*, and *wha's*.

[20] Kautzsch (2002), however, provides strong evidence that combining of *is* and *are* is not warranted in analyses of earlier phases of AAE.

[21] Over time, other researchers have argued for various modifications of the envelope of variation established by Labov. Bailey and Maynor (1985a) and Poplack and Sankoff (1987) argued for the inclusion of copula/auxiliary forms following *it*, *that*, and *what*, pointing out that in their data clear instances of zero occurred after these. Poplack and Sankoff also included 1st singular tokens in their corpus since zero comprised 10 percent of the data there, while Bailey and Maynor calculated zero as a percentage of all copula forms, arguing that the breadth of its occurrence in their data made it difficult to view zero copula/auxiliary solely as the result of a deletion process that operates on the output of contraction. None of these other proposals, however, has gained the widespread acceptance that Wolfram's has.

Table 2 Token types usually excluded from the envelope of variation in studies of zero copula/auxiliary.
(The order in the table generally reflects the frequency with which forms are excluded from the envelope of variation. Shaded boxes are universally excluded. See Rickford et al. [1992] and Blake [1997] for a list of studies that exclude token types that are not shaded.)

Token Types	Example	Reason Given for Exclusion
Infinitive forms	He jus' *wanna be* aroun' me.	Not contractable or deletable
Past copula forms	They *was* still talkin' about it on TV.	Not contractable or deletable
ain't	Your heart *ain't* that bad.	Not contractable or deletable
Before sibilants	*She* (*'s*/0) scared of Aunt Betty.	-*s* neutralized by following sibilant
Clause final	She won't tell me how ol' she *is*.	Not contractable or deletable
Emphatic	Mama that hotel *is* AMAZING!	Not contractable or deletable
Invariant *be*	They *be* tellin' that girl what to do.	Not contractable or deletable
1st person	*I'm* trying not to eat too much today.	*I'm*/*am* is invariant; not deleteable
Questions	Where *0* her shoes at? *Are* yall there?	Word order creates different contraction/deletion processes
Negatives	*She's not* like most people.	Word order creates different contraction/deletion processes
it, that, what	*It's* gettin' hot in here.	Assibilation yields *i's, tha's, wha's*; deletion does not occur
Existential *there*	*There's* three or four more people.	*There's* is suppletive
Where *are* occurs[a]	They *0* from Wal-Mart.	Result of desulcalization rather than deletion

[a] Most people now include these in the envelope of variation.

generally, and for a comprehensive review of early work on zero copula).[22]
Table 2 summarizes the environments included and excluded from the envelope

---

[22] There were also suggestions for changes in methods of calculating contraction well, with "straight contraction" calculating contracted forms as a percentage of full, contracted, and deleted forms (C/F +C+D). Romaine (1982) offers still a different approach, positing that deletion takes place before contraction. Her deletion calculation is essentially the same as straight deletion, but for her, contracted forms are simply a percentage of full plus contracted forms (C/F+C).

of variation typically used in analyzing zero copula once the modification suggested by Wolfram was made.

It is important to note a crucial (and usually unstated) implication of this envelope of variation and more generally of the argument that zero is the result of a phonological process that is simply an extension of copula/auxiliary contraction. If zero results from a sequence of phonological processes (i.e., is the result of deletion operating on the output of contraction), its origin need not be sought in any source language: rather, it can be explained simply as a consequence of internal phonological operations within AAE itself. The significance of the envelope of variation to this argument cannot be overstated here: if one accepts the envelope of variation that is typically used in the analysis of zero, then deletion operating on the output of contraction is the simplest and most straightforward explanation for zero. While a number of researchers have argued that zero most likely arose from the substrate languages that were crucial in the initial formation of AAE (see, for example, Baugh 1980; Blake 1997; Holm 1984; Rickford 1998; and Rickford et al. 1992), in their work they have generally continued to use (or assume) the envelope of variation described here, basing their arguments solely on the effects of the following predicate on the occurrence of zero. With the exception of Blake (1997), none of them has addressed the effects that the structure of the envelope of variation might have on conclusions that can be reached regarding zero. However, it is the envelope of variation typically used for analyzing zero that makes deletion the best explanation for the occurrence of zero and thus makes external sources (including input languages) unnecessary. And it is the envelope itself that needs to be reexamined.

Using Blake (1997) as a starting point, this Element reexamines the envelope of variation used for analyzing zero and explores whether or not other structures should be part of that envelope. Our reexamination demonstrates that several typically excluded structures should in fact be included, and it then proposes a model that includes them. When they are made part of the envelope of variation, it becomes clear that zero cannot be the product of a deletion process that operates on the output of contraction (or, for that matter, any deletion process at all) and that its origins must be sought in the sources that gave rise to AAE. Further, the analyses used to revise the envelope of variation provide insights into some factors influencing the occurrence of zero that have not been discussed elsewhere (Cukor-Avila 1999 is an exception). Those factors, in turn, help us identify subtle but critical changes that took place in the distribution of zero over the course of the twentieth century, changes which, when taken in conjunction with developments in be_2, suggest a restructuring in the AAE copula/auxiliary system.

4.2 Determining What to Count in the Analysis of Zero

Table 3 summarizes the 29,000+ copula/auxiliary forms in Table 1 according to their place inside or outside the envelope of variation most often used for the analysis of zero.[23] Perhaps the most striking thing about Table 3 is that even with both 3rd singular and plural/2nd singular included, as Wolfram (1974) and many researchers subsequent to him have done, the forms that most often comprise the envelope of variation for the analysis of zero make up only a little over a third of the total corpus of finite, present tense, copula/auxiliary forms. Negatives and questions, both of which are typically excluded from databases used to analyze zero, comprise about 13 percent of the corpus, while another roughly 16 percent of the copula/auxiliary tokens in our corpus are 1st

Table 3 Summary of copula/auxiliary forms in the Springville corpus according to their place in the traditional envelope of variation for zero copula. (3rd sing. and plural/2nd sing. totals are combined; nonfinite forms, past copula forms, *ain't*, and forms before sibilants are excluded; shaded boxes include other forms that are often excluded.)

	Total Number of Tokens	Percent of Total Corpus ($N = 29,459$)
Copula forms in traditional envelope of variation	10,769	36.56
Invariant *be* (all environments)	1,312	4.45
1st sing. (excluding *be*)	4,693	15.93
Emphatic/clause final (excluding *be*, 1st sing.)	823	2.79
Questions (excluding *be*, 1st sing.)	3,117	10.58
Negatives (excluding *be*, 1st sing., emphatic/clause final, questions)	818	2.78
what, it, that subjects (excluding *be*, emphatic/clause final, questions, negatives)	7,751	26.31
Existential *there* (excluding *be*, emphatic/ clause final, questions, negatives)	176	0.60

---

[23] Again, we treat *ain't* as a single negating morpheme here (it deserves its own independent analysis) and *-s* before sibilants is almost always ambiguous.

person forms, also excluded from the envelope of variation. Invariant *be*, again typically excluded, accounts for a little over 4 percent of the tokens, while emphatic and clause final tokens comprise an additional 2.79 percent. Finally, forms following *what*, *it*, and *that* (WIT forms), which are also usually excluded, make up more than a quarter of the corpus. As Blake (1997: 58) has pointed out, "when one considers that [don't count] copula tokens can be as numerous as or several times more numerous than count tokens, their importance for quantitative analyses of the copula looms even larger."

Even so, eliminating the forms that are typically excluded might not be a problem. As Wolfram (1969:166) notes, "in the quantitative measurement of copula absence, it is essential to separate environments where there is no variability from those where there is legitimate variation between the presence and absence of the copula. Failure to distinguish these environments would skew the figures of systematic variation." The question, then, is not so much the total number of forms that occur in the "don't count" environments, but rather whether there is legitimate variation between overt copula/auxiliary forms and zero in those environments. To help determine the scope of legitimate variation between zero and explicit copula/auxiliary forms, the third column in Table 4 summarizes zero as a percentage of all forms in each of the environments in Table 3. As Table 4 shows, while zero accounts for 59.73 percent of the forms in contexts that make up the typical envelope of variation, it also comprises 42.54 percent of the of the forms with questions (this figure includes WIT questions) and 23.11 percent of the forms with negatives (including a substantial number of WIT negatives). Zero clearly is not an alternative for invariant *be*, is negligible in clause final/emphatic environments, and is quite rare as a percentage of 1st person singular tokens. However, it accounts for more than 16 percent of the tokens with existential *there* and comprises close to 5 percent of the tokens following WITs (WITs in negatives and questions are included with those structures rather than with WITs). Separating those contexts in which there is legitimate variation between zero and overt copula forms from those in which there is not, then, is less straightforward than it might appear at first glance. Zero is obviously more frequent in structures that comprise the traditional envelope of variation than it is elsewhere, but it is also a viable copula/auxiliary alternative in questions and negatives and is more than negligible, though not especially frequent, following WITs (a total of 345 zero forms occurs after WITs) and existential *there*. From a theoretical perspective, there may be reasons for eliminating these four environments from the envelope of variation, but the first two especially and probably the third and fourth cannot be eliminated

Table 4 Zero as a percentage of all forms in each of eight contexts, and zero within each context as a percentage of all zero forms. (3rd sing. and plural/2nd sing. totals are combined; nonfinite forms, past copula forms, *ain't*, and forms before sibilants are excluded; shaded forms include other forms that are often excluded.)

	Total Number of Tokens in Each Context	Total Number of Zero Tokens in Each Context	Zero as a Percent of Total Tokens in Each Context	Zero as a Percent of Total Number of Zero Tokens ($N = 8396$)
Copula forms in traditional envelope of variation	10,769	6,432	59.73	76.61
Invariant *be* (all environments)	1,312	—	—	—
1st sing. (excluding *be*)	4,693	61	1.30	0.73
Emphatic/clause final (excluding *be*, 1st sing.)	823	14	1.70	0.17
Questions (excluding *be*, 1st sing.)	3,117	1,326	42.54	15.79
Negatives (excluding *be*, 1st sing., emphatic/ clause final, questions)	818	189	23.11	2.25
what, it, that subjects (excluding *be*, emphatic/ clause final, questions, negatives)	7,751	345	4.45	4.11
Existential *there* (excluding *be*, emphatic/clause final, questions, negatives)	176	29	16.48	0.35

solely because of a lack of legitimate variation – zero is a viable alternative in all four environments.

Two other considerations are also important in evaluating the consequences of eliminating various "don't count" structures from the envelope of variation. First, the structures within which there is significant variation between zero and overt copulas/auxiliaries are not necessarily the same for all populations. Poplack and Sankoff (1987) indicate that zero accounts for 10 percent of the 1st singular tokens in their Samaná data, and in the data from the former slaves, the percentage of 1st person singular zero forms is roughly twice that in the Springville corpus (see Bailey and Maynor 1989). The envelope of variation for diaspora varieties or for a diachronic analysis of zero copula, then, might well be different from that in the synchronic analysis here.

Second, and perhaps more important, excluding some of the contexts most often categorized as "don't count" not only substantially reduces the total corpus of copula/auxiliary forms, but it also eliminates a significant number of zero forms themselves. As the fourth column in Table 4 also shows, almost a quarter of the 8,396 zero forms in the Springville corpus occur in contexts that are typically eliminated from the envelope of variation. While deletion that operates on the output of contraction provides an elegant, sophisticated explanation for three-quarters of the zero tokens in the corpus, nearly one in four zero tokens (1,964 instances of zero in the Springville corpus) remains unaccounted for if that approach is used. It may be that these residual tokens occur as the result of a different process (or processes), but that has not been shown to be the case. In fact, studies of zero usually just ignore the residual zeros even though they may be a substantial percentage of the total number of zero forms in the corpus.

The fact that zero occurs with some frequency outside the typical envelope of variation does not mean that the envelope of variation typically used is incorrect: that envelope, and the phonological process of deletion that it implies, may well be the right analysis for the three-quarters of the zero tokens that it includes. It is important to remember, though, that the conclusions that have been reached about zero in previous work, including conclusions about the factors that influence its occurrence, are valid not for the full range of zero forms in a corpus, but only for the "contractable" ones – about 75 percent of the corpus. In light of the issues that this creates for the Principle of Accountability (see Rickford 1986), however, it is crucial that we determine whether any of the "don't count" environments, and particularly those that include substantial numbers of residual zeros, belong in the envelope of variation. In addition, it is important to explore the implications that any modifications to the envelope might have for the conclusions that can be reached about zero and about its origins.

We approach this problem by examining the consequences of expanding the envelope of variation for the analysis of zero copula to exclude only (1) those contexts in which zero never occurs or (2) those contexts in which zero represents less than 2 percent of the total number of tokens and hence is clearly not a productive alternative. Given these criteria, the "don't count" contexts would comprise only emphatics, clause final forms, *ain't*, invariant *be*, 1st person singular, past tense, and forms before sibilants, as in examples 19 to 25.

19. She *is* running things!
20. I bet you don't know who this *is*.
21. It *ain't* too far from here.
22. You *be wastin'* your money just to buy 'em toys.
23. *I'm* gonna plan some music real quick. / *I am* very, very, very happy
24. He *was* there Saturday.
25. *He's so* cute.

In applying this revised envelope of variation to present tense copula/auxiliary forms in the Springville corpus, we also excluded 191 forms (including 45 zeros) that were ambiguous or could not be classified with any certainty. After this adjustment, the revised envelope of variation for the Springville corpus, which comprises questions, negatives, WITs, and existentials as well as forms in the typical envelope of variation, includes 98.76 percent of the 8,396 zero copula forms (all but 104). Further, the database that results from this revised envelope comprises roughly 77 percent of the total Springville copula/auxiliary corpus. Thus, in meeting the Principle of Accountability (i.e., ensuring that as many zero forms as possible are included in the analysis), the revised envelope of variation is clearly superior to the traditional one. However, the question of whether questions, negatives, and WITS actually belong in the same envelope with "deletable" forms is still unresolved.

Perhaps the best way to determine whether these structures all belong in the same envelope of variation is to examine the factors that influence the occurrence of zero in them. If the factors that promote or inhibit zero in questions, negatives, and WITs are substantially the same as those that promote or inhibit zero in the traditional envelope of variation, then it seems reasonable to conclude that the zeros in those structures belong in the same envelope of variation as "deletables." Substantial differences among the factors would call for different envelopes of variation and different explanations for those zeros not in the traditional envelope.

The focus here is on the two predictor variables that a vast body of research has shown to have the greatest influence on the occurrence of zero in the traditional envelope of variation: its subject type and its predicate type

(Bailey and Maynor 1985a; Baugh 1980; Blake 1997; Holm 1984; Labov 1969, 1972b; Poplack and Sankoff 1987; Rickford 1998; Rickford et al. 1992; Weldon 2003; and Wolfram 1974). A personal pronoun subject (other than *it*) favors zero, while an NP subject other than a personal pronoun disfavors it. Among predicates, a hierarchy of favoring and disfavoring predicates exists: *gonna* and present participle (v+*ing*) predicates favor zero copula, while NP predicates disfavor it, with predicate adjectives and locatives/adverbs falling somewhere in between. To assess how different subject and predicate types affect questions, negatives, and WITs, we compare their effects on zero in those structures with their effects on zero in the traditional envelope of variation using the binary logistic regression procedure discussed in Section 2.3. To isolate the effects that questions and negatives have independently on zero, the initial statistical analysis sets aside the WITs used in questions and negatives, as in examples 26 and 27.

26. Is *it* ready now? / Where *that* gonna be at?
27. *That's* not cool at all.

For that reason, the percentages of zero for questions and negatives given in the analysis are slightly higher than the percentages given in Table 3. (The WITs used in questions and negatives, however, are included in the revised model for analyzing zero that we present later in this Element). In addition, in the analysis we have combined existentials with WITs since the corpus includes only 176 existentials and because existentials overlap with WITs through the use of the existential *it* that occurs in AAE. Finally, in the analysis here we have combined tokens of the pre-verbal *fixin' to* with the *gonna* tokens. There are too few tokens of *fixin' to* to analyze separately, and the frequency of zero in them is virtually identical to that of *gonna*.

4.3 How Many Envelopes of Variation?

The results of the binary logistic regression analysis of subject and predicate type on zero in the traditional envelope of variation provide both a benchmark for comparing the analysis here with other studies of zero copula/auxiliary and also a baseline for determining whether WITs, negatives, and questions should be included in the envelope of variation used for the analysis of zero. Blake (1997), Rickford (1998), and Rickford et al. (1992) provide convenient summaries of the factors that promote and inhibit zero in the traditional envelope of variation in a large number of studies of AAE. Their summaries show a remarkable consistency among the effects of the two predictor variables most often used, subject type and predicate type. As we have seen, almost

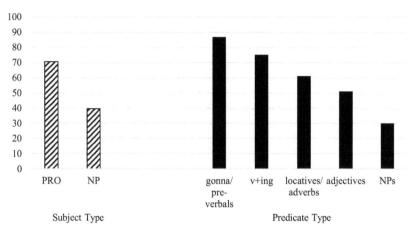

Figure 5 Effect of subject and predicate type on zero in the traditional envelope of variation. (Zero as a percentage of all forms in each environment: N=10,698 excluding ambiguous predicates).

without exception a personal pronoun subject (other than *it*, of course) favors zero, while other subjects favor full and contracted forms. Again, in every case they examine, *gonna* and v+*ing* predicates strongly favor zero, while NP predicates disfavor it, with adjectives and locatives falling somewhere in between.

Table 5 summarizes the results of the binary logistic regression analysis of zero in the traditional envelope of variation in the Springville data in the following way. Within each predictor variable, each indicator's strength is shown using the odds ratio associated with the dependent variable in relation to its respective reference (NP for subject type and adjective for predicate type). An odds ratio of 1.0 means there is no relationship between an indicator within a predictor variable and the dependent variable. An odds ratio greater than 1.0 means there is a positive relationship, while an odds ratio less than 1.0 means there is a negative one. The odds ratios thus enable us to infer the relative effects of personal pronoun versus NP for subject type and to infer a hierarchy of relative effects for predicate type. Figure 5 gives information on the percentages of zero in the relevant predictor environments.

As the odds ratios in Table 5 show, the Springville data is quite consistent with results of other studies of zero in AAE. Regarding subject type, the odds ratio for a pronoun subject is 3.564, showing a strong positive relationship between pronouns and zero. The relationship with the reference (NP), of course, is negative. Regarding predicates, the odds ratios show a hierarchy of positive associations that is identical to the hierarchy in other studies. For *gonna*, the

Table 5 Odds ratios for the occurrence of zero copula/auxiliary by subject type and predicate type in the traditional envelope of variation (R^2 = 25.7 percent).

	PRO	NP (constant)	gonna/Pre-verbals	v+ing	Locatives/Adverbs	Adjective (constant)	NP
Subject type[a]	3.546	0.667					
Predicate type[b]			6.184	2.901	1.573	1.037	0.405

[a] For subject type alone, R^2 = 11.2 percent

[b] For predicate type alone, R^2 = 21.3 percent

odds ratio is 6.184, for v+*ing* it is 2.901, and for locatives it is 1.573.[24] On the other hand, the association between zero and NP predicates is negative (0.405): NP predicates clearly disfavor zero forms (adjectives are the reference here).

The binary logistic regression analysis also provides a measure of the amount of variation in the corpus explained by the predictor variables. As Table 5 shows, taken together to comprise the full model, the predictor variables explain 25.7 percent of the variation, a strong R^2 for data in the social sciences. Viewed independently, predicate type explains significantly more variation than subject type does: predicate type independently explains 21.3 percent of the variation in the corpus, while subject type explains only 11.2 percent. Although there is no definitive study proving that predicate type has a greater impact on zero copula than subject type, the focus of much of the work on zero has been on the predicate type, something which suggests that most researchers believe that the predicate has the greater impact; the R^2 in this study lends support to that belief.[25]

The evidence from the traditional envelope of variation, then, provides a point of reference which demonstrates that zero in Springville operates just

---

[24] One way of understanding the magnitude of the odds ratio is to look at how much more likely zero is than the constant in each environment: for *gonna* the odds ratio of 6.184 means that zero is 518.4 percent more likely to occur than with the constant (i.e., adjectives), while the odds ratio for v+*ing* of 2.901 and for locatives of 1.573 make zero 190.5 percent and 57.3 percent more likely to occur in those environments, respectively. On the other hand, the odds ratio for NP predicates of 0.405 makes zero 59.5 percent less likely to occur than with the constant.

[25] See Rickford (1998, 2015) for an extensive discussion of the importance of the following environment, especially for creolist arguments. While the order of predicate effects in AAE generally matches those in creoles, Rickford and others have noted that the relative order of adjectives and locatives in AAE sometimes presents problems for the "creole origins" hypothesis. In creoles, adjectives (which are verbs) favor the occurrence of zero more strongly than locatives do, but in studies of AAE the relative effect of adjectives and locatives on zero varies quite a bit. Two things should be considered here, however. First, the relationship between locatives and verbs is complex and may play a role in the fact that while locatives do not pattern with the more verb-like predicates in their effects on zero, neither do they pattern with NPs (or even adjectives). As Hengeveld (2011) notes, locative nonverbal predications can be a source from which aspectual categories (and particularly the progressive) develop. Further, Comrie (1976: 99) points out that "in older stages of the English language, one form of the Progressive was overtly locative, with a verbal noun preceded by a locative preposition." The a-prefix, which was used in earlier AAE as well as earlier White varieties (see Cukor-Avila and Bailey 2015), is a relic of this locative-progressive relationship. In light of the role that locatives played in the development of the progressive, the steady intermediate place of locatives in the hierarchy of effects on zero makes some sense. Second, the category of adjective in English is quite complex and includes both verbs used as adjectives (past participles) and also the stativity distinction that occurs with English verbs. As we show in this Element, each of these subcategories affects the occurrence of zero differently. Because there may be different proportions of each adjective subcategory in a given corpus, especially if the number of tokens in the corpus is relatively small, it should not be surprising to find that adjectives affect zero differently in different corpora. Given these complexities, variation in the relative effects of adjectives and locatives on zero are not unexpected.

like zero in virtually every other study of the form in AAE. It also provides a clear baseline of predictor variable effects for assessing whether the zeros in WITs, negatives, and questions belong in the same envelope of variation with the zeros usually included there or whether they belong in a different one.

Tables 6 and 7 summarize the results of the binary logistic regression analysis of zero in questions, negatives, and WITs, with results from the traditional envelope included for comparison. Figures 6 and 7 provide the percentages of zero in each environment. Note that no analysis of subject type is included for WITs in Table 6 since there are no other subjects for comparison in that structure, and the analysis of predicates in negatives includes an additional category for *not*, which can occur alone with no predicate following. Also, the negative corpus excludes tokens of *ain't*, *never*, and the three tokens of negative contraction in the corpus (as in *a chicken isn't too smart*).[26] As the odds ratios, which can only be compared within columns, in Tables 6 and 7 show, with just two exceptions the hierarchies for both subject and predicate type are the same for questions, negatives, and WITS as they are for structures in the traditional envelope of variation. In every case, pronoun subjects favor zero and NP subjects disfavor it, while *gonna* and v+*ing* predicates promote zero and NP predicates disfavor it, with locatives and adjectives lying somewhere in between. The only exceptions, and both are minor, involve one instance each in negatives and WITs, where adjectives more strongly disfavor zero than NPs do. It is important to note here, though, that because *ain't* is excluded, the corpus of negatives includes only 481 tokens, of which just 59 are NPs and just 96 are adjectives (compare this to the next smallest data set, for questions, with 2,201 tokens and more than two and a half times as many adjectives). This discrepancy, then, may be the result of the relatively small number of tokens for negatives. The discussion of WITs provides a possible explanation for the discrepancy in that structure. Even with these minor differences, though, it is clear that the same factors that promote and inhibit zero in the traditional envelope of variation also promote and inhibit it in questions, negatives, and WITs. These similarities provide strong evidence for including questions, negatives, and WITs in a single envelope of variation for analyzing zero.

---

[26] Negation in English is made more complex by the option of two types of contraction that may occur, in addition to full forms and, in some dialects, *ain't*. Auxiliary contraction (as in *a chicken's not too smart*), the only type of contraction possible with nonnegatives, occurs when the copula or auxiliary attaches to a preceding noun or pronoun. Negative contraction occurs when *not* attaches to the preceding copula or auxiliary (as in *a chicken isn't too smart*). As Pérez (2013) points out, auxiliary contraction is far more common with copula and present tense *be* auxiliary forms than negative contraction is, and further, auxiliary contraction seems to be expanding at the expense of negative contraction for these forms. In our corpus of more than 2,500,000 words, negative contraction appears only three times, so we have excluded it here. As pointed out, we excluded *ain't* because we treat it as a single negating morpheme.

Table 6 Odds ratios for the occurrence of zero copula/auxiliary by subject type in questions and negatives. (Traditional envelope is included for comparison; WITs are not included because they have only WIT subjects.)

	Questions	Negatives	Traditional
PRO	2.646	2.069	3.546
NP (constant)	0.773	0.329	0.667

Table 7 Odds ratios for the occurrence of zero copula/auxiliary by predicate type in questions, negatives, and WITs. (Traditional envelope is included for comparison.)

	Questions	Negatives	WITs	Traditional
gonna/pre-verbals	4.400	2.691	4.314	6.184
v+*ing*	2.924	1.806	4.243	2.901
Locative/adverb	2.040	1.420	0.601	1.573
Adjectives (constant)	0.797	0.415	0.050	1.037
NP	0.405	0.952	0.729	0.405
not	—	0.542	—	—

Two factors still might seem to weigh against including all four structures in the same envelope of variation, however: differences in the amount of variance explained for each structure and differences in the frequency with which zero occurs. Table 8 provides the R^2 for the analyses summarized in Tables 6 and 7. As Table 8 shows, in every case R^2 is higher for predicate type than for subject type, suggesting that, as in the traditional envelope, predicate type explains more of the variance in the data than subject type. Nevertheless, while the overall R^2 is only slightly lower for questions than for structures in the traditional envelope of variation, it is a good bit lower for negatives and WITs, suggesting that the model explains much less of the variation for the latter two. It is important to remember, though, that the predictor factors used here were developed for the traditional envelope of variation and have not been modified to account for the grammatical differences that characterize the other structures. This discussion suggests ways that the predictor factors can be modified so that the model becomes a good fit for all four structures under consideration here.

The frequency differences in the occurrence of zero between the traditional envelope and WITs and negatives in particular may also create reservations

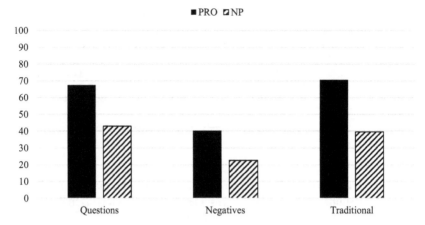

Figure 6 Effect of subject type on zero: Zero as a percentage of all forms for questions (N=2201 excluding WIT subjects and tag questions) and negatives (N=481 excluding WIT subjects, never, and negative contraction). Traditional (N=10,698 excluding ambiguous predicates) included for reference.

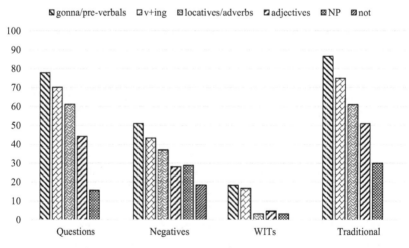

Figure 7 Effect of predicate type on zero: Zero as a percentage of all forms in each environment for questions (N=2201 excluding WIT subjects and tag questions), negatives (N=481 excluding WIT subjects, never, and negative contraction), and WITs (N=7674). Traditional (N=10,698 excluding ambiguous predicates) included for reference.

Table 8 R^2 in questions, negatives, and WITs with the traditional envelope included for comparison.

	Questions	Negatives	WITs	Traditional
Full model summary	22.1%	8.5%	5.4%	25.7%
Subject type	7.1%	2.4%	–	11.2%
Predicate type	22.0%	7.0%	5.4%	21.3%

about including all four structures in the same envelope of variation. While zero comprises 59.73 percent of the forms in the traditional envelope of variation and 42.54 percent with questions, it comprises only 23.11 percent with negatives and 4.45 percent with WITs. A more detailed look at WITs and negatives will help explain these frequency differences and show why they are less important than they might at first appear.

A close examination of the WIT tokens themselves suggests that the relatively low frequency of zero in these structures is at least partly a consequence of differences between WITs and the traditional envelope in the distribution of tokens among the various predicate types. The distribution of the 10,698 tokens in the traditional envelope of variation by predicate type is as follows (see Figure 8): 1,870 tokens before *gonna/pre-verbals* (17.48 percent); 2,536 tokens before v+*ing* (23.71 percent); 2,210 tokens before NP (20.66 percent); 1,330 tokens before locatives/adverbs (12.43 percent); and 2,752 before adjectives (25.72 percent). Contrast this with the distribution of the 7,674 WIT tokens: only 263 tokens before *gonna* (3.43 percent) and 216 tokens before v+*ing* (2.81 percent), but 5,147 tokens before NP (67.07 percent), 465 tokens before locatives (6.06 percent), and 1,583 (20.63 percent) before adjectives. What is immediately clear from these numbers is that the vast majority of WIT tokens (more than two-thirds) occur before an NP, the environment that most strongly disfavors zero, in contrast to the traditional envelope of variation, where only about a fifth of the tokens occur before an NP. Moreover, only 6.24 percent of the WIT tokens occur before *gonna* and v+*ing*, the predicate types that most strongly promote zero, in contrast to 41.19 percent of the tokens that occur in these environments in the traditional envelope. The small percentage of zero tokens in WIT constructions, then, can be explained to some degree by the fact that most of the WIT tokens in the corpus occur in environments that strongly disfavor zero.

But these figures actually understate the issue. Cukor-Avila (1999) has shown that especially among people born after World War II, the subtype of

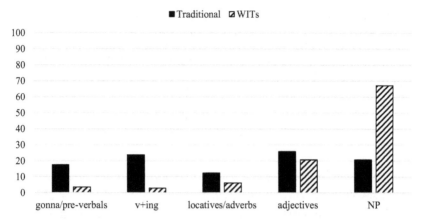

Figure 8 Distribution of tokens by predicate type in the traditional envelope of variation (N=10,698 excluding ambiguous predicates) and WITs (N=7674 excluding questions, negatives, and ambiguous predicates).

predicate adjective has a significant effect on the occurrence of zero: non-stative adjectives strongly favor zero, operating much like v+*ing*, while stative adjectives strongly disfavor zero, operating more like NPs (the discussion of adjective subtypes in Sections 4.4 and 4.5 on the revised model and on twentieth-century developments provides additional confirmation of Cukor-Avila's finding). A look at the distribution of tokens within adjective subtypes in the traditional envelope of variation and among WITs also shows a pattern that strongly disfavors zero in the latter. In the traditional envelope of variation, 64.14 percent of the adjectives are statives (1,765 of the 2,752 adjective tokens). Among WITs, however, a little more than 85 percent of the adjective tokens are statives (1,349 of the 1,583 tokens). Again, a substantially greater percentage of WIT tokens occur in environments that strongly disfavor zero.

Combining stative adjectives with NP tokens, on the one hand, and non-stative adjectives with *gonna* and v+*ing*, on the other, throws the discrepancy among favoring and disfavoring environments between WITs and the traditional envelope into sharp relief. As Figure 9 shows, in the traditional envelope, stative adjectives and NPs combined account for 37.16 percent of the 10,698 tokens, while *gonna*, v+*ing*, and nonstative/participials account for 47.27 percent. Contrast this with WITs: NPs and statives account for 84.65 percent of the 7,674 WIT tokens, while *gonna*, v+*ing*, and nonstative/participials account for only 9.29 percent. In light of the distribution of tokens

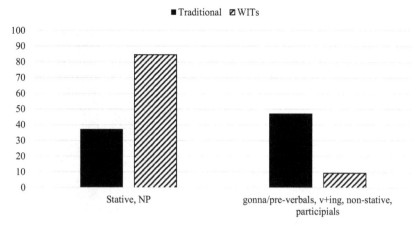

Figure 9 Distribution of tokens by stativity in the traditional envelope of variation (N=10,698 excluding ambiguous predicates) and WITs (N=7674 excluding questions, negatives, and ambiguous predicates).

by following environment, it is not at all surprising that the frequency of zero among WITs is quite low.

But even this understates the issue. Although since Wolfram (1974) most researchers have combined plural/2nd person singular forms with third singular forms in the analysis of zero, there is nevertheless a quantitative difference in how the person/number of the subject affects the occurrence of zero, with zero occurring at a substantially higher rate when the subject is plural or 2nd person singular (see Bailey and Maynor 1985a and 1985b). The Springville data shows this same quantitative difference: zero occurs with 51.94 percent of the 3rd singular subjects in the traditional envelope of variation but with 72.46 percent of the plural and 2nd singular subjects. In the traditional envelope, plural and 2nd singular subjects account for a little more than a third of the data – 38.22 percent of the total number of tokens (4,089 of 10,698); 3rd singular accounts for 61.78 percent (6,609 tokens). Contrast this with the person/number distribution of WIT subjects: only 0.51 percent (39) of the 7,674 WIT tokens have plural/2nd singular subjects (many of these are existential *they's*); 99.49 percent occur with 3rd singular subjects (see Figure 10). Again, the discrepancies in the distribution of tokens are a factor in the differences in the frequency of zero between the traditional envelope of variation and WITs.

Given the fact that the vast majority of WIT tokens are third singular and occur with predicate types that disfavor zero, it is not surprising that the

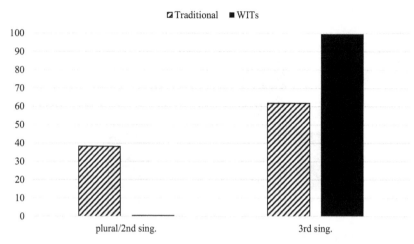

Figure 10 Distribution of tokens by person/number in the traditional envelope of variation (N=10,698 excluding ambiguous predicates) and WITs (N=7674 excluding questions, negatives, and ambiguous predicates).

frequency of zero with WITs is quite low.[27] The situation with negatives is somewhat different in that the distribution of tokens in negatives is much like that in the traditional envelope of variation. However, the difference that Cukor-Avila (1999) found between the effects of stative and nonstative adjectives provides a cue here, as does a comparison of the differences between the traditional envelope and negatives in the frequency of zero among the various following predicate types.

Interestingly, the differences between the traditional envelope and negatives in the frequencies of zero are particularly dramatic for those predicate types that most often promote zero in the traditional envelope. Figure 11 shows the differential between the frequency of zero in negative constructions (always *not* in this corpus) and in the traditional envelope of variation by predicate type. As Figure 11 shows, before *gonna*, and v+*ing*, the frequency of zero is reduced by roughly a third in negative constructions, and it is reduced by more than 20 percent before locatives and nonstative adjectives. Before NPs, however, *not* has virtually no effect on the frequency of zero, and the differential for stative

---

[27] We are not suggesting here that the distributional differences in tokens by predicate and subject type are responsible for all of the frequency differences between WITs and the tokens in the traditional envelope of variation. In fact, it is clear that WITs themselves play a role as well. A detailed analysis of that role and of all the frequency differences between WITs and the traditional envelope is outside the scope of this Element, though.

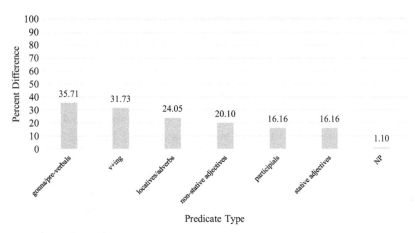

Predicate Type

Figure 11 Differential in the use of zero between negatives and the traditional envelope of variation: Zero as a percentage of all forms in each environment in negatives (N=481 excluding WIT subjects, never, and negative contraction) and in the traditional envelope of variation (N=10,698 excluding ambiguous predicates).

and participial adjectives is only about 16 percent. The pattern in the frequency differences between zero in negatives and in the traditional envelope suggests that the differences are most likely a consequence of the semantics of *not*. Remember that in the traditional envelope zero occurs most often with actions, much less so with states. From this perspective, negatives have a much greater impact on actions than on states since they actually turn actions into states, as a comparison of examples 28 and 29 shows:

28. She's eating that cornbread. (action)
29. She's not eating that cornbread. (state)

Thus, since a negative turns an action into a state, it is not at all surprising that negatives show lower frequencies of zero than the traditional envelope and that much of the difference lies in the frequencies before *gonna* and v+*ing*, the forms that signal actions.

Given the similarities in the effects of predictor variables between the traditional envelope and questions, negatives, and WITs and the explanations provided here for the dramatic differences in the frequency of zero among the structures, it seems quite reasonable to include all four structures in a single envelope of variation for the analysis of zero. Further, in light of the discussion of frequency differences, it should also be clear that the predictor variables should be modified as well. The revision of the envelope and the predictor variables provide a new model for the analysis of zero in AAE, one that better meets the Principle of Accountability (Rickford 1986) and that explains a remarkably high amount of the variance in the data.

4.4 A Revised Model for Zero

The inclusion of questions, negatives, and WITs along with tokens in the traditional envelope of variation provides a database from the Springville corpus of 22,458 tokens for the analysis of zero, a database that (1) includes about 77 percent of the total number of copula/present tense of *be* tokens in the Springville corpus (1st person singular, invariant *be*, clause final/ emphatic forms, and 3rd singular forms before sibilants comprise the remaining 23 percent) and (2) excludes only 104 (1.24 percent) of the 8,396 zero forms. To examine the factors that promote or inhibit zero in this expanded database, we use the same binary logistic regression procedure described in Section 2.3. In addition, we use an all-possible-regression procedure with backward elimination to determine how much of the variance in the data each of the predictor variables explains independently, and how much those variables explain independently when grouped in all possible combinations. Based on the analysis in Section 4.3, the revised model uses the following as predictor variables: (1) subject type, which includes WITs as a separate subject subtype alongside NPs and personal pronouns excluding *it*; (2) predicate type, which includes stative adjectives, nonstative/participial adjectives, and final *not* as separate predicate subtypes along with *gonna*, v +*ing*, locatives and other adverbs, and NPs (because of the separation of adjective subtypes, we use locatives as the reference variable or constant in the analysis); (3) person/number of the subject, which includes 3rd singular on the one hand and plurals/2nd person singular on the other; and (4) sentence type, which includes questions, negatives, and the positive statements that comprise the traditional envelope of variation.

Tables 9 and 10 summarize the results of the all-possible-regression procedure with backward elimination and the binary logistic regression respectively on the four predictor variables. As Table 9 shows, the revised model explains 52.7 percent of the variance in the Springville copula corpus, more than twice the amount of variance (25.7 percent) explained by the model for the traditional envelope of variation (remember that the model had less explanatory power for the other three structures). While an R^2 of 25.7 percent is acceptable in the social sciences (see Freedman 2009), one that explains more than 50 percent of the variance is obviously quite powerful. The strong R^2 is an excellent argument for a model that (1) includes WITs, negatives, and

Table 9 All-possible-regression with backward elimination for the revised model.

Predictor Variable(s)	Percent of R^2 Variance Explained	Percent Change in R^2
Full model	52.7	–
Person/number; subj. type; pred. type	52.1	–0.06
Person/number; subj. type; sent. type	46.3	–6.4
Person/number; pred. type; sent. type	40.3	–12.4
Subj. type; pred. type; sent. type	52.4	–0.03
Person/number; subj. type	45.7	–7.0
Person/number; pred. type	39.6	–13.1
Person/number; sent. type	19.5	–33.2
Subj. type; pred. type	51.9	–0.08
Subj. type; sent. type	45.5	–7.2
Pred. type; sent. type	36.0	–16.7
Person/number	19.1	–33.6
Subject type	44.9	–7.8
Predicate type	35.4	–17.3
Sentence type	0.8	–51.9

questions along with tokens in the traditional envelope and (2) includes the expanded set of predictor variables described previously.[28] The revised model is clearly a good fit for the data.

Although some increase in the amount of variance explained should be expected with the increase in the number of predictor variables and the sample size that emerges from the expanded database, as Table 9 shows, almost all of the increase actually occurs within the two predictor variables that were used in the original model – subject type and predicate type. Sentence type independently explains less than 1 percent of the variance, but the person/number of the subject explains 19.1 percent of the variance in the corpus. While this is less than what is explained by subject and predicate type, it is still a considerable amount of variance. Person/number of the subject is obviously a predictor of the occurrence of zero, but as we will see, much of what it explains, about

---

[28] It is important to note here also that situational and social variables have not been considered in this analysis. Their inclusion should further increase the explanatory power of the model.

Table 10 Odds ratios for the occurrence of zero copula/auxiliary in four predictor variables in the revised model (full model R^2 = 52.7 percent).

Subject type (R^2 = 44.9 percent)	Odds ratio
Pronoun	3.221
NP (constant)	0.678
WITS	0.073
Predicate type (R^2 = 35.4 percent)	
gonna/pre-verbals	3.542
v+*ing*	2.466
Nonstative/participial adjectives	1.319
Locatives/adverbs (constant)	0.894
Stative adjectives	0.381
not	0.170
NP	0.138
Person/number of the subject (R^2 = 19.1 percent)	
Plural/2nd sing.	6.462
3rd sing. (constant)	0.354
Sentence type (R^2 = 0.08 percent)	
Questions	2.616
Positive statements	1.930
Negatives (constant)	0.299

98 percent, is not independent of subject type. In the original model, subject type (i.e., the grammatical category of the subject as opposed to its person/number) explained 11.2 percent of the variance among tokens in the traditional envelope of variation, but in the revised model, this predictor variable explains 44.9 percent of the variance. The large increase in explanatory power is due primarily to the inclusion of WIT as a subject type. Based on the hierarchy of predictive factors that influence zero in WITs and the fact that zero accounts for almost 5 percent of the WIT tokens, it seems clear that they belong in the envelope of variation for the analysis of zero. The data here, however, suggests that WIT subjects themselves also significantly inhibit the occurrence of zero, but the goodness of fit of the revised model is a strong argument for their inclusion.

Finally, predicate type, the most important explanatory variable in the original model, explained 22 percent of the variance in the traditional envelope of variation. In the revised model, with adjectives subdivided into nonstative/participials and statives and with *not* treated as a separate subcategory when it occurs alone as a result of ellipsis, predicate type explains 35.4 percent of the variance, again a large increase in explanatory power. The important factor here is the separation of adjectives into subtypes. *Not* occurring alone represents a very small proportion of the data and is thus not particularly important in accounting for the variance in the data. The division of the adjective indicator into two categories has a much broader effect, however. Adjectives account for 22 percent of the data, and as shown, the two adjective indicators have very different effects. As the R^2 shows, with the modifications of the subject type and predicate type predictor variables, the expansion of the corpus to include questions, negatives, WITs, and the inclusion of all but 104 of the 8,396 zero forms, the revised model not only represents a significant improvement in accountability for zero, but it also provides an excellent fit for the data.

Table 9 also shows how predictor variables in all possible combinations explain independent R^2. Subject and predicate type combined explain 51.9 percent of the independent R^2 – virtually all (about 98.5 percent) of the explained variance in the data. The addition of person/number combined with subject and predicate type, only increases the explained independent R^2 by 0.02 percent, and the addition of sentence type increases it by only 0.58 percent. The fact that subject and predicate type combined, then, provide almost all of the independent explanation of variance in the data provides strong justification for the focus on these two variables in the prior literature on zero and suggests that the model probably should be further revised to exclude the sentence type and person/number predictor variables. Their inclusion provides only a minimal increase in explanatory power.

The data summarized in Table 10 enables us to rank order the effects of the various indicators within each predictor variable in the revised model. As the odds ratios in Table 10 show, within subject type, the odds of zero occurring with pronouns is quite high (3.221) but extremely low with WITs (0.073), even lower than with the constant (NP). Within predicate type, the same hierarchy that appears in other studies of zero copula emerges here, but the separation of nonstative/participial adjectives from statives and the use of *not* as a separate indicator when it occurs without a following predicate provide additional insight into what is happening. Note that because of the separation of adjective subtypes, locatives/adverbs were used as the reference (constant) in the revised model. In the revised model, the greatest odds for the occurrence of zero with predicate subtypes is with *gonna* (3.542), followed, in turn, by v+*ing* (2.466) and nonstative/participial adjectives (1.319). Zero is negatively associated with the other indicators for predicate type: stative adjectives (0.381), NPs (0.138), and *not* (0.170). What seems to be happening here is exactly what Cukor-Avila (1999) suggested: more verb-like predicates favor zero, while more noun-like ones disfavor it. Note that locatives/adverbs are negatively associated with zero in the revised model. As expected, for the person/number predictor variable, zero is positively associated with environments where other varieties of English have *are* (6.462) and negatively associated with environments where they have *is* (0.354). Both positive statement (1.930) and question (2.616) indicators are positively associated with zero in sentence type, although interestingly enough, the odds ratio for questions is actually higher than for positive statements. Keep in mind, however, that while all the indicators in person/number and sentence type are statistically significant, neither predictor variable has a great deal of independent explanatory power and could easily be eliminated from the model.

The revised model, then, accounts for a much larger percentage of the total copula corpus than the original model does, accounts for virtually all of the zero forms in the corpus, and explains more than half of the variance in the data, an extremely large amount for behavioral data. Questions, negatives, and WITs obviously belong in the envelope of variation. Moreover, it seems clear that adjective subtype should be accounted for in the analysis as well. Finally, it also seems clear that person/number and sentence type can be removed from the model with virtually no loss of explanatory power.

4.5 Developments in Zero during the Twentieth Century

The revised model, which includes virtually all of the zeros in the corpus and explains a high amount of variance in the data, also has important implications for the sources of zero in AAE. Since questions and negatives do not meet the criteria for contraction, present tense zero copula/auxiliary cannot be the product of deletion that operates on the output of contraction. In fact, it is hard to see how zero can be the product of any deletion process at all given the variety of environments in which it occurs. Further, the fact that the occurrence of zero is strongly influenced by the following predicate suggests that its lineage cannot be traced to varieties of English in any way. Rather, its source must be either in the African or creole languages that served as part of the input to AAE or in some second language learning process. While an exploration of the precise origins of zero is outside the scope of this Element, zero is clearly inherited from something other than English. What is within the scope of this Element, though, are the twentieth-century developments in this inherited feature.

Most research on zero in twentieth-century AAE has assumed that it is one of the most stable features of the variety and that zero has changed little since its emergence. An examination of both the overall frequency of zero in apparent time in the twentieth century and its frequency with the predictor variables used in the traditional model for zero suggests just that, as Figure 12 shows. The lack

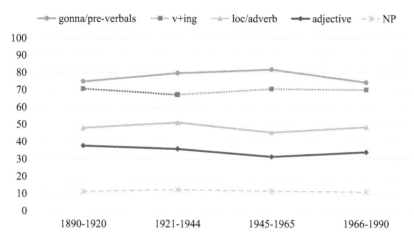

Figure 12 Effect of predicate type on zero in apparent time in the traditional model: zero as a percentage of all forms in each environment.

of variation from generation to generation shown here is remarkable; this is about as close to a flat line as any apparent time distribution comes.[29] But this apparent stability is misleading in two ways. First, Kautzsch (2002) has shown that the use of zero was evolving throughout the nineteenth century and most likely did not stabilize until near the end of that century. Second, broad grammatical categories such as *adjective* can obscure subtle developments that may have significant grammatical consequences. An examination of zero using the predictor variables in the revised model tells a somewhat different story from that depicted in Figure 12. In light of the differences in the effects of stative and nonstative adjectives already described, we examined their effects in apparent time to determine whether they showed stability as well. In this analysis we also separated participial adjectives from nonstatives and statives.

As Figure 13 shows, while apparent time distributions among *gonna*, v+*ing*, locatives, and NP change very little, the situation with adjective subcategories is far from stable. Among the oldest generation, nonstative and stative adjectives are similar in their effect on the occurrence of zero (at 37.25 percent and 32.30 percent respectively). The frequencies of occurrence for zero with both lie somewhere in between that of NPs and locatives. In the second oldest generation, this situation begins to change as the frequency of zero before nonstatives increases substantially to 55.10 percent, exceeding that of locatives. The change accelerates among the two

---

[29] Zero is also quite stable in the individual vernaculars of Springville adults, as Cukor-Avila and Bailey (2013) demonstrate. It shows no evidence of either age-grading or life-span change.

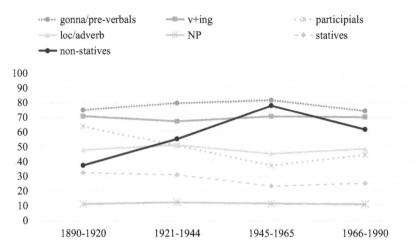

Figure 13 Effect of predicate type (including adjective subtypes) on zero in apparent time in the revised model: zero as a percentage of all forms in each environment.

youngest generations so that the frequency of zero more closely aligns with that of v+*ing* and *gonna* than of locatives. At the same time, the frequency of zero before statives moves slightly in the opposite direction, declining from about 32 percent among the oldest respondents to about 25 percent among the youngest. Perhaps even more surprising is what happens with participial adjectives. Among the oldest respondents, the frequency of zero with participials is 63.64 percent, more like that with v+*ing* than that with stative and nonstative adjectives. Among the youngest two generations this alignment changes dramatically: the frequency of zero with participial adjectives is lower than the frequency with locatives. What seems to be happening here is a reanalysis of the role of zero within the copula/auxiliary system.

Among the oldest generation, the occurrence of zero correlates largely with the "verbness" of the predicate, with high rates of zero occurring before *gonna*, v+*ing*, and participial adjectives (which are, after all, verbs used adjectivally) and lower rates appearing before both stative and nonstative adjectives and before NPs, with locatives somewhere in between, as Figure 13 shows. This begins to change in the second oldest generation, and by the youngest generation the occurrence of zero correlates most closely with the "nonstativeness" of the predicate, with high rates of zero clustering among *gonna*, v+*ing*, and nonstative adjectives, all categories that are dynamic or reflect actions as opposed to states (again, see Figure 13). Just as be_2 was reanalyzed to become a marker of durative/habitual contexts, zero seems to have been reanalyzed so that instead of marking "verbness," it comes to mark "nonstativity." We should point out that the correlations between adjective subcategory and zero described here are not shown in any other study except for Cukor-Avila (1999). However, it is not that other studies have found contradictory evidence; it is simply that they have not looked for differences among adjective subcategories. We believe that, had the analysis in other studies been done in the same way that ours was, they would have found the same results. After all, as the analysis here of forms in the traditional envelope of variation shows, when we looked at the copula/auxiliary in the way that others have, we obtained the same results. Likewise, our analysis of invariant *be* provides results that are similar to those in other studies. In other words, in every other way, the evidence from Springville mirrors that in other studies of AAE. We have no reason to believe that it does not do so for adjective subcategories as well.

The reanalysis of zero so that it marks "nonstativity" accounts for several seeming anomalies in the data. First, it explains not only why the occurrence of zero increased dramatically before nonstative adjectives, but also why it declined before participial adjectives – they are typically stative, as in examples 30 and 31:

30. Like you make it outta that cotton wood stuff, like puff wood or whatever.
    That floor is made with that. [f/1939/1994]
31. *That car is parked* in there too straight. [f/1978/1997]

Second, it explains the low frequency of zero with negatives (note that the frequency of zero before negatives, 23.11 percent, is quite similar to that before stative adjectives). Third, it helps explain the low frequency before WITs. As we point out, 84.65 percent of the WIT tokens occur before NPs or stative adjectives.

The best explanation for the correlation of zero with various adjective subcategories in apparent time in the Springville data, then, is that zero underwent a reanalysis over the course of the first half of the twentieth century and as a result, came to mark not the verbness of the predicate, but rather its nonstativity. The similarities to the restructuring of invariant *be*, discussed in Section 3, are striking. In fact, a comparison of Figure 13 with Figures 2 to 4 suggests that even the timeframes for these restructurings are similar. Those similarities call for further analysis.

5 The Interaction of Innovation with Inheritance in the Twentieth-Century AAE Copula/Auxiliary System

To summarize, during the twentieth century, the Springville AAE present tense copula/auxiliary system evolved in some remarkable ways. At the beginning of the century, the copula/auxiliary included five forms – *am*, *is*, *are*, *be*, and zero – that overlapped significantly in their distributions and functions. The person/number of the subject generally governed the first three, although *is* was also used sometimes in the plural and second singular as well as the third singular, especially after NP subjects (see Bailey, Maynor, and Cukor-Avila 1989). The latter two forms, however, were just alternatives for the first three, although zero typically did not occur in 1st person and its occurrence was influenced both by the form of the subject (personal pronoun subjects except for *it* favored zero) and also by the form of the predicate (the more verb-like predicates, i.e., *gonna*, present participles, and past participles, favored the occurrence of zero). By the last quarter of the century, each of these alternative forms had developed a unique function: *be* had evolved into a durative/habitual marker within the present tense copula/auxiliary system and zero had come to be used primarily with nonstative or dynamic predicates in that system (nonstative adjectives favored its occurrence almost as strongly as *gonna* and v+*ing* did). A closer look at the contexts within which these changes took place will help identify some of the factors that most likely triggered and promoted them.

5.1 Triggers for the Changes in *be*$_2$ and Zero During the Twentieth Century

It is important to note that the evolution of invariant *be* and zero in twentieth century AAE followed a period of significant change and restructuring in the present tense copula/auxiliary system of English more generally. As Baugh and Cable (2012) point out, the widespread expansion in the use of progressive forms in English began in the seventeenth century and extended into the nineteenth until it approximated current usage. Tagliamonte (2013) suggests that the grammaticalization and extensive use of *be+going+to* (*gonna*) as a future in English evolved over a similar timeframe, though as she notes, it continues to spread in some varieties (see also Tagliamonte, Durham, and Smith 2014). As late as the eighteenth and nineteenth centuries, then, the English present tense copula/auxiliary system was still evolving, completing the development of new aspectual and tense distinctions even as it finished sorting out the configuration of the paradigm, with *are* replacing *be* as a plural form in most varieties (Bailey 1989). In some respects, then, the development of invariant *be* as a durative/habitual marker and zero as a marker of nonstativity can be seen simply as an extension of the overall formal and functional evolution of the present tense copula/auxiliary system. The flux in the larger system itself was at least a contributing factor in the restructuring of the AAE copula/auxiliary system.

The flux in the system, of course, does not explain specifically why *be* became a durative/habitual marker and zero came to correlate with nonstativity. The specific trigger for the former was most likely related to developments in the second type of invariant *be*, the one derived from *will/would* deletion. Three factors are especially relevant here. First, *would be* (and hence invariant *be* derived from *would* deletion) functioned (and still sometimes functions) as a past habitual, as in example 32; *will be* (and invariant *be* from deleted *will*) can sometimes carry habitual meaning as well, as in example 33. When invariant *be* resulted from *would* and *will* deletion, it also often carried habitual meaning, as in examples 34 and 35.

32. My cousin was tellin' that sometime *they'd be sittin'* on the porch an' see a snake come wanderin' up in the yard an' they'd have to jump up an' get the gun an' shoot it. [f/1912/1988]
33. I can drive up there a lotta time an' mos' of the time *I'll be* in the truck an' sometime *I'll be* in that little ol' uh, whatever you call them, you know they cars that boy got. [m/1932/1992]
34. I used to, when the kids, when I worked over there on weeken', *some of us be sick*, see I had to shell all that money outta my pocket. [f/1961/1992]
35. Now he'll get up five, six thirty an' *he be outside* doin' somethin'. I'll be sleepin'. [f/1941/1994]

Second, it is important to keep in mind the substantial ambiguity and overlap between *be* derived from *will/would* deletion and durative/habitual *be*. In fact, it is often difficult to distinguish between the two, as examples 36 and 37 show.

36. If you hadn't been I'd been out doin' somethin' right now. That's right. I just had put the truck up down here an' put it over there out there. Usually *I be down there* doin' something. [m/1913/1994]
37. It's ten thirty-five. Usually *you be at work* at eleven. [f/1996/2018]

Third, *would be* (and invariant *be* derived from deleted *would*) had a competitor for the function of past habituality for several centuries, and during the twentieth century the competitor won out. Even as *gonna* was being grammaticalized as a future in English, *useta* was being grammaticalized as a marker of past habituality. Although *used to* as a past habitual in English (grammaticalized over time as *useta*) goes back to late Middle English/Early Modern English, its diffusion took place over several centuries. As late as the twentieth century we see its continuing spread in AAE. In Springville, *useta* accounted for only 44 percent of all past habituals among the oldest residents, with *would be* and invariant *be* derived from *would* deletion accounting for the remainder. Among the next oldest age group, however, the occurrence of *useta* expanded dramatically at the expense of *would be* and *be* derived from deleted *would*: in the second oldest age group, *useta* accounts for 69 percent of the past habitual tokens. It continues to expand among the youngest generation, where it accounts for more than 72 percent of the past habituals. This expansion of *useta* as a past habitual occurs not only at the expense of *would be* but also at the expense of invariant *be* derived from *would/will* deletion, as Figure 1 shows.

The growth in the frequency of be_2 and the expansion of its use as a durative/habitual marker in the present tense closely tracks both the expansion of *useta* as a past habitual and also the decline of invariant *be* derived from *will/would*. As the use of durative/habitual be_2 increases, its nondurative/nonhabitual use declines until it becomes miniscule. Figure 14 plots both the decline of invariant *be* derived from *will/would* deletion and the rise of be_2 as a durative/habitual at the expense of nondurative/nonhabitual uses. When these three developments are viewed together, what has happened seems clear. As *useta* expanded as a past habitual, *would be* and invariant *be* derived from *would* deletion decreased dramatically in their frequency. As that happened, the habituality associated with invariant *be* derived from *would* (and sometimes *will*) deletion came to be associated with be_2 in the present tense, something that was likely triggered by the ambiguity that often existed between invariant *be* derived from deleted *will/would* and be_2. As a result, over time, be_2 came to serve as a marker of habituality (and durativity, especially when used with statives) in the present tense copula/auxiliary. As be_2 became a marker of durativity/habituality, the AAE copula/auxiliary system developed greater transparency and an association between form and function that was much closer to a one-to-one relationship (Langacker 1977). Even as most varieties of English were creating greater transparency in the copula/auxiliary system by simply eliminating be_2, AAE was creating greater transparency by reanalyzing the form so that it became a durative/habitual marker within that system. This grammaticalization of be_2, then, simply offered a different pathway to greater transparency, one that provided formal marking of an aspectual distinction that must be marked periphrastically in other varieties.

Although invariant *be* derived from *will/would* deletion does continue to occur among the younger residents of Springville, it is rare, as is the use of be_2 in nondurative/nonhabitual contexts (see Figure 14 and also the discussion in Section 3). Among those residents, *useta* is well established as the predominate past habitual (with *would* relegated primarily to its other functions, e.g., as an irrealis), while be_2 is well established as the predominate habitual in the present copula/auxiliary system. The working out of the association of these grammatical functions with particular grammatical forms illustrates clearly the interplay between innovation and inherited features. AAE inherited both

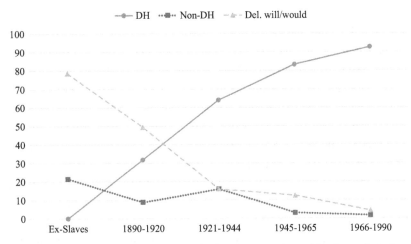

Figure 14 Distribution of invariant *be* in apparent time. (Totals exclude 1st person singular).

a copula/auxiliary paradigm and a system of marking past habituality that lacked a clear one-to-one relationship between form and function. The copula/auxiliary had five forms to mark three person/number distinctions, with two of those forms having no particular person/number relationships. The past habitual had two formal mechanisms for marking it, one a single grammatical form and the other a periphrastic construction. The expansion of the single grammatical form *useta* at the expense of the periphrastic *would be* (and invariant *be* derived from *would* deletion) allowed be_2 to assume the meaning of habituality that invariant *be* from *would* deletion carried, and as be_2 assumed that meaning as part of the present tense copula/auxiliary paradigm, it created greater transparency within that paradigm, providing a specific function for a form that did not have one. Innovation (through the grammaticalization of be_2 as a habitual marker), then, not only changed the function of an inherited form, but it also created a more transparent paradigm than the one that was inherited.

Like be_2, zero is an inherited feature that has changed over the course of the twentieth century, but it differs in some important ways. First, its source obviously does not lie in English dialects. While creolists have sometimes fretted over the precise order of predicate effects, and especially over the relative order of predicate adjectives and predicate locatives, the fact that the predicate has any effect at all indicates that zero was inherited from something other than English and is a strong argument for a connection with either creole or African antecedents.[30] Further, the analysis in Section 4 eliminates the possibility that zero might be the result of a deletion process, something that would remove the need for any source language. Both the Principle of Accountability and strong parallels in the effects of the following environment on the occurrence of zero require the inclusion of questions, negatives, and WITs in the envelope of variation for zero. Once those forms are included, the model for zero becomes quite powerful and explains a remarkably high amount of variance in the data (with just subject type and predicate type included as explanatory variables, the model has an R^2 of 51.9 percent). Just as important, though, their inclusion eliminates the possibility of deletion as an explanation for zero. Zero is best understood, then, as an inherited feature whose source was in something other than English.

Second, zero differs from be_2 in that the changes in its use are not immediately obvious. At first glance, zero seems remarkably stable, as Figure 12 suggests. It is only when adjective subcategories are separated in the apparent time analysis that it becomes clear a change is underway (see Figure 13). The reversal of the effects of zero on participial adjectives, which favored zero in the oldest age group but not in the two younger ones, and on nonstative adjectives, which disfavored zero in the oldest age group but favored it in the two younger ones, confirms that while the distribution of zero was driven by the form of the predicate (i.e., its verbness) at the beginning of the twentieth century, by the end of the century it was driven by the dynamic or nonstative nature of the predicate. The persistence (and perhaps acceleration) of these effects among Springville residents who came of age in the twenty-first century provides confirmation that the change is ongoing. As Figure 15 shows, among these residents, the occurrence of zero with nonstative adjectives is almost equal to the occurrence with v+*ing* forms, while the use of zero with stative adjectives is only six percentage points greater than that with NPs. Further, the use of zero with participials continues to decline and is below 30 percent among the youngest Springville cohort. Although the reanalysis of zero as a marker of nonstativity is not as complete as the reanalysis of be_2 as a marker of durativity/habituality, the trend is quite clear.[31]

Third, unlike with be_2, the triggers for the reanalysis of zero are not obvious at first glance. Several factors may have played a role, however. For one thing,

---

[30] See the discussion of the issue in Rickford (1998).

[31] The trends that developed with be_2 in the twentieth century also continue with those who came of age in the twenty-first. Not only does the form occur as frequently with this group as it does with the youngest generation represented in Figure 14, but the distribution of various types of invariant *be* is almost identical: 93.58 percent of the invariant *be* tokens are durative/habituals, with only 2.75 percent derived from *will/would* deletion and 1.83 percent representing non-durative/nonhabitual uses of the be_2 tokens.

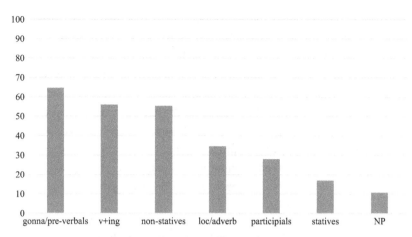

Figure 15 Zero copula/auxiliary by predicate type for Springville residents born
1991–2002: zero as a percentage of all forms in each environment.

significant overlap already existed between the form of the predicate and the stative/
nonstative distinction within the copula/auxiliary system. The predicates that
historically have favored zero, v+*ing* and *gonna*, are both dynamic, while NPs
and stative adjectives, of course, reflect states. From this perspective, exactly what
the correlate of zero is – predicate type or nonstativity – is somewhat ambiguous. It
is only within the adjective category that stativity comes into play independently,
and of course that is precisely where the change takes place. The shift from
predicate type to stative/nonstative aspect was thus an easy and perhaps
a disambiguating one. In addition, the shift from predicate type to aspect as the
correlate of zero occurred within a more general context of aspectual development.
The progressive itself was a relatively late development, and *useta* was still in the
process of becoming the most common past habitual marker during the first
decades of the twentieth century. Perhaps more important, the contemporary
emergence of a marker of durative/habitual aspect in the AAE present tense
copula/auxiliary system provided further emphasis on aspectual distinctions. The
shift in the primary correlate of zero from the form of the predicate to nonstative
aspect, then, occurred within the context of, and was perhaps in part motivated by,
a more general shift in focus to aspectual distinctions.

The reanalysis of *be₂* and zero that took place over the course of the twentieth
century clearly demonstrates the interplay of innovation on inheritance.
Inherited forms can sometimes be reanalyzed to take on new functions as
a way of resolving ambiguity and providing transparency. In both of the cases
here, the mismatch (and ambiguity) between form and function was resolved in
AAE not by eliminating forms, as in most varieties of English, but by

reanalyzing them so that they developed new functions. The reanalyzed features provide a grammatical form, in both cases a reanalyzed inherited form, to signal an aspectual distinction that had been either signaled by the use of an adverb or that had simply been implied in the form of the predicate. The reanalysis of these inherited forms, in turn, leads to a larger restructuring of the present tense copula/auxiliary system in AAE. By the last forty years or so of the twentieth century, the AAE copula/auxiliary system was not only marked for person/number and progressive aspect, as in most varieties of English, but was also marked for durative/habitual aspect (by be_2) and, except in the 1st singular, for stative aspect (with *is/are* used primarily for statives and zero for nonstatives).

5.2 The Sociocultural Contexts for Change

In the reorganization of its present tense copula/auxiliary system, AAE showed the kind of fundamental restructuring that characterizes New Englishes during their Nativization Phase, the phase that is "at the heart of the birth of a new, formally distinct [language]" (Schneider 2007: 44). Although the sociocultural and demographic forces that helped shape AAE are different from those that affect many other PCEs, it is clear that during the twentieth century, AAE saw significant restructuring as a consequence of the interplay between innovation and inherited forms and that this interplay helped lead to a distinct variety with widespread use by African Americans across the United States. With a few exceptions, the pathways of innovation documented here have not been discussed elsewhere in the literature (see Bailey and Maynor 1987 for such an exception), although a number of studies have demonstrated that the features that are the end products of those pathways are used pervasively in AAE across the United States and thus are part of the core of this formally distinct variety.

While the discussion here documents the pathways of innovation and reanalysis that led to the restructuring of the AAE present tense copula/auxiliary system, it does not show the sociocultural and demographic mechanisms by which these developments became prevalent across a broad swath of the United States. Bailey and Maynor (1987) suggest that the development of be_2 took place within the context of the most important population movement among African Americans in the twentieth century – the Great Migration.[32] The Great Migration, which began during World War I and continued into the 1970s, was a movement of African

---

[32] There was a "Great Migration" of Whites out of the rural South into Northern cities as well. In fact, a larger number of Whites left than Blacks, although as a percentage of the total population the migration of African Americans was greater. In addition, the migration of African Americans and its consequences are better documented and studied. The cultural dislocation and isolation

Americans out of the rural South into cities, primarily in the urban North.[33] Bailey and Maynor (1987:19–20) summarize the situation as follows:

> In 1890, 90 percent of the [African American] population lived in the South, and 80 percent lived in rural areas. Twenty years later, 89 percent was still in the South and less than 25 percent was in cities. With the advent of World War I, however, [African Americans] began moving in large numbers to cities and to the North, responding to increasing economic opportunity there, decreasing economic opportunity in the South (the consequences of the boll weevil, fluctuation in cotton prices, and technological innovation), and the desire to escape racial discrimination. By 1970, the results of this massive shift in the population were clear: 47 percent of the [African American] population lived outside the South, while 77 percent lived in cities, with 34 percent of the [African American] population concentrated in seven major urban centers: New York, Chicago, Detroit, Philadelphia, Washington, D.C., Los Angeles, and Baltimore . . .. The migration of [African Americans] was not just to cities but to inner city areas. As Jones (1980) points out, the settlement of [African Americans] in inner cities extended from the earliest years of the Great Migration to the present. By 1960, over half of the [African American] population lived in inner cities; in 1976, that figure had risen to nearly 60 percent.

The consequences of the Great Migration led to more than just the redistribution of the African American population, however. It also stimulated a massive cultural surge in African American music, literature, and thought as jazz and its offshoots became the most popular music in the United States and perhaps in the world; as a literary renaissance emerged in Harlem (one of the primary destinations of the Great Migration); and as African American newspapers became thought leaders in the fight against racism and oppression. These forms of cultural expression helped create a unique cultural identity as well, and an ideal context for the emergence of a distinct variety.[34]

---

that migration to Northern cities caused among Whites are well documented in country music of the 1960s and 1970s, with the best example being Bobby Bare's "I Want to Go Home."

[33] There is an extensive literature on the Great Migration, especially as it affects African Americans. A few of the more pertinent studies here include Gregory (2006), Groh (1972), Hamilton (1972), Jones (1980), Lehmann (1991), Smith (1966), and Wilkerson (2010). Bailey and Maynor (1987) provide a convenient summary of demographic data on the Great Migration; we draw heavily on that in this Element.

[34] Although most scholars recognize that durative/habitual *be* is an innovation in AAE, there is some disagreement about the timeframe during which it arose. For instance, using examples of *be*+v+*ing* in the BLUR corpus, Miethaner (2014) argues that the innovative use of this form may have begun during the last decades of the nineteenth century, before the Great Migration began. It may well be that the association of habituality with be_2 began earlier than Bailey and Maynor (1987) suggested: even among the oldest Springville residents, durative/habitual uses of be_2 comprise around 30 percent of the invariant *be* tokens. This evidence, and that from the BLUR corpus, however, should be evaluated in light of several other factors. The first is simply the dramatic expansion in the number of instances of be_2 in apparent time. Among the oldest Springville residents, be_2 accounts for less than 2 percent of the data. Its occurrence nearly

How this variety became widely used across a vast territory in a relatively short timeframe, however, is another matter. It is not a unique problem though. Labov (2012: 112) points out that the spread of the Northern Cities Shift creates a similar problem of diffusion:

> It is evident that no local mechanism can be driving the Northern Cities Shift in the same direction with the same results over this vast area. If there is a social motivation that is involved in this long-term and widespread process, it cannot depend on face-to-face contact between the speakers involved.

There are similar problems in explaining the rapid diffusion both of quotative *be like* (see Tagliamonte, D'Arcy, and Louro 2016 and D'Arcy 2021) and of features such as *fixin to* and the *pen/pin* merger in Southern American English as well (see Bailey 1997). In the case of the former, *be like* spread in Englishes around the world, used in much the same way and with similar constraints, in widely separated, seemingly unconnected places over three to four decades. In the case of the latter, a number of grammatical and phonological features spread across the American South, an area with few large cities and relatively limited interregional communication networks, over a roughly sixty-year period from 1880 to World War II. In neither case could mechanisms of face-to-face contact have been the driving force.

While face-to-face contact could not have been the driving force in the spread of the restructured copula/auxiliary system of AAE either, several factors likely aided its diffusion. First, as African Americans moved into northern cities beginning around World War I to form new, dynamic communities, they came from a shared cultural hearth in the rural South. As Bailey (2001) points out, although different patterns of slavery existed along the Atlantic Coast in the Upper and Lower South during the colonial period, with the invention of the cotton gin those patterns coalesced as slavery spread rapidly westward as far as the Brazos River in Texas. Within fifty years of the

---

doubles in the next generation, the first to come of age during the Great Migration, and increases by another 40 percent among the last generation to come of age during the twentieth century. The increase is especially striking among Springville residents born after 1920 and nicely parallels the increase in the use of *be$_2$* to mark habituality. The second factor is the ambiguity between durative/habitual *be* and *be* derived from *will/would* deletion. As we note in several places in this Element, the two types of *be* are difficult to distinguish from each other, especially among older residents, who used *be* derived from *will/would* deletion much more often than younger generations. The third factor is the possibility of life span changes. As we point out in Section 2.3, it has become increasingly clear that during their life spans, individuals may adjust their vernaculars in the direction of innovations in the community grammar. As a result, the data from older generations can sometimes overstate the use of innovative features and lead researchers to conclude that those innovations began earlier than they actually did (cf. Sankoff 2018). The best hypothesis, then, still seems to be that the feature emerged and began to spread around the beginning of the Great Migration.

invention of the cotton gin, large-scale farming of short-staple cotton using slave labor came to dominate in the area south and west of the Appalachian Mountains with similar patterns of slaveholding.[35] In response to the expansion of cotton production, the African slave trade grew dramatically: by far, the largest number of slave importations into the United States came in the two decades after 1780. Further, legislation taking effect in 1808 to end the international slave trade did not end it: more slaves were imported between 1808 and 1860, when the African slave trade was illegal, than before 1730. During this period, however, the importation of slaves from abroad was dwarfed by the expansion of the domestic slave trade, with slaves being sold and transported from the Atlantic Coast to the Interior South in shocking numbers. It is estimated that more than a million African Americans were forcibly moved westward. In proportional terms, this represents one of the largest demographic movements in American history. In the trans-Appalachian South, then, the demographic mix and the similarities in the plantations organized around cotton production created a kind of monoculture across a broad region.

Second, although the Civil War ended slavery, the reorganization of the former plantations into large farms with former slaves becoming tenants, most often sharecroppers, ensured that the cultural, economic, and social patterns that existed before the war were preserved after it. These patterns were fixed into law with the passage of Jim Crow legislation, especially after 1890, throughout the South. Further, with wide fluctuations in cotton prices and natural ravages such as the boll weevil, tenant farming, and especially sharecropping, eventually led to a kind of debt peonage. Grinding poverty was often the result.[36] Combined with the legal constraints that made social mobility and equality under the law almost impossible and with the brutal repressive measures used to enforce all of this, that poverty provided the ideal stimulus for migration away from the South. The labor shortages created by the military service of factory workers in the North in World War I created a "pull" mechanism for migration to Northern cities (and later to cities on the West Coast as World War II saw another round of labor shortages) that

---

[35] The discussion that follows is based on Bailey (2001). Bailey includes a number of useful tables and figures that provide details on the foreign and domestic slave trade, on plantation sizes, and on population ratios. That paper also provides a perspective both on African and creole influences in phonology and on phonological features that seem to have developed independently. See Thomas and Bailey (1998) for additional evidence on African and creole influences in phonology.

[36] See Agee and Evans (1941). While the focus of their book is largely on White sharecroppers, almost all of what they find applies to African American sharecroppers as well. As Bailey (2001) points out, White farmers became tenants and sharecroppers only slightly less often than African Americans did.

complemented the "push" mechanism of the Southern socioeconomic context.

Finally, as Bailey and Maynor (1987: 468) point out, the migration northward and westward generally followed three broad streams: "movements from the South Atlantic states to Northeastern cities, from the East South-Central states to North Central cities, and from the West South-Central states to Western and Midwestern cities." They also note, though, that a fourth stream of migration developed later, after the initial stream of migration from South to North: an inter-metropolitan movement connected major destination cities in the Great Migration with one another. In addition, migrants to the Northern cities often maintained their ties to the areas from which they migrated.

These demographic developments had important consequences for the emergence of the linguistic innovations described in this Element. The creation of a broad monoculture across the trans-Appalachian South meant that African Americans moving to the north most likely shared a linguistic ecology that was receptive to and even promoted the innovations described in Section 5.1. As D'Arcy (2021) notes, a shared linguistic ecology may have been the key to the emergence of quotative *be like* in widely separated geographic areas in the same way at the same time; a shared ecology was almost certainly part of the stimulus for durative/habitual *be* and zero as a marker of nonstativity. Further, the emergence during the Great Migration of a limited set of migration streams from source areas in the South, the maintenance of ties to those areas after the migration began, and the interurban migration streams that also developed produced communications networks that allowed the products of African American culture, including language, to eventually spread around the nation. Taken together, the shared linguistic ecology, the distinct cultural identity, and the communication networks that developed out of the Great Migration provided an ideal context for the development and diffusion of linguistic innovations and thus the creation of a "new formally distinct language" during the first fifty years or so of the twentieth century.[37]

6 Conclusion

Most of the vast literature on AAE has focused on its uses, its structure, and its origins. The neglected topic in this literature is the history of AAE – how it has

---

[37] Although the focus here is only on present tense copula/auxiliary *be*, other work suggests that several additional innovations, such as *had*+past used as a simple past and *ain't* used for *didn't*, developed within AAE in a similar timeframe. See Cukor-Avila (1995, 2001) and Cukor-Avila and Bailey (1995b) for discussions of the former and Fisher (2018), and Smith (2018) for discussions of the latter.

evolved and developed over the more than 300 years that African Americans have been in the United States. Part of the neglect, of course, is simply a consequence of a lack of evidence. People who are forbidden from learning to read and write can hardly leave behind the written documents on which linguistic history is usually based, so we are unlikely to ever discover the kind of data on the oldest varieties of AAE that would allow us to understand its early historical development very well. By the middle of the twentieth century, though, evidence on the language of African Americans had become plentiful, and some of that evidence (e.g., the slave narratives analyzed in Schneider 1989, the HOODOO texts analyzed in Ewers 1996, the transcriptions of recordings with former slaves provided in Bailey, Maynor, and Cukor-Avila 1991, and the comparative analyses of all these sources in Kautzsch 2002) were almost certainly accurate depictions of earlier varieties of AAE. The assumptions that underlie the apparent time construct allow us to infer from these sources what AAE in the middle of the nineteenth century might have looked like.[38] However, most contemporary field studies have focused on obtaining synchronic descriptions of AAE, especially of the speech of children, teenagers, and young adults. The focus on younger African Americans made it difficult to examine possible changes in apparent time that might show precisely how the variety was developing (or had developed) during the twentieth century. The Springville Project was designed to fill that gap.

Using data from the Springville Project, our apparent time analysis of two iconic AAE features, invariant *be* and zero copula/auxiliary, suggests that they underwent some remarkable developments over the course of the twentieth century. Those developments demonstrate (1) how innovation operates on inherited forms to create new grammatical distinctions and (2) how those new distinctions can lead to restructuring within a linguistic subsystem, in this case the present tense copula/auxiliary. That restructuring, in turn, illustrates the kind of linguistic processes that take place during the "Nativization" stage in the creation of PCEs, the stage during which a new language is created. It is processes like these that have made AAE distinctive enough so that some refer to it as a language rather than a dialect, as AAL rather than AAE.

---

[38] The essays in Bailey, Maynor, and Cukor-Avila (1991) use that data, sometimes along with other sources, to make inferences about what nineteenth-century AAE might have looked like. See Bailey and Thomas (1998) for an analysis of some of the vowel systems in the slave recordings and Kautzsch (2002, 2012), Poplack (2000), Poplack and Tagliamonte (2001), and Schneider (1989) for more comprehensive overviews of earlier AAE.

The reanalyses of invariant *be* and of zero also suggest some of the kinds of contexts that likely promote grammatical reanalysis (and hence linguistic restructuring) more generally. Those contexts include:

(1) mismatches between form and function (in this case in inherited features). A mismatch in the present tense copula/auxiliary system already existed with invariant *be*, which simply served as an infrequent alternative for *are* and to a lesser extent *am* and *is* in the English sources of AAE. The mismatch was exacerbated by the inheritance of zero from non-English sources as another alternative for *are* and *is*.

(2) grammatical ambiguity beyond the form and function mismatch. A second type of invariant *be*, this one derived from the deletion of an underlying *will* or *would* and often signaling past (and sometimes present) habituality, created significant grammatical ambiguity with be_2. The two types of invariant *be* were not always distinguishable in their use: the formal equivalence between the two was matched by functional overlap. In the case of zero, the source of the ambiguity may in part be differences in form classes between creoles (creolization is the likely source for zero in AAE) and English. In many creoles, adjectives are verbs (see, for example, the discussion in Bickerton 1981, Holm 1988, Rickford 1998, and Romaine 1988), and creoles typically do not require a copula before verbal predicates. The occurrence of zero in the data of the oldest Springville residents shows a pattern suggestive of creoles. As Figure 12 demonstrates, *gonna*, v+*ing*, and participial adjectives all group together in strongly favoring zero even as other adjective subcategories favor *is/are*. Over time, this configuration changes, but the change is not simply a movement toward English norms, which would lead to the loss of zero altogether. Rather, zero persists, with the distinction between stative and nonstative aspect, which applies to adjectives in English and is implicit in the full range of predicates in the present tense copula/auxiliary, becoming the primary factor promoting zero. As Figure 13 shows, among younger Springville residents it is *gonna*, v+*ing*, and nonstative adjectives that favor zero, with participial adjectives functioning more like locatives. While other studies have not yet identified or confirmed either this change or the role that stativity plays in the AAE copula/auxiliary, we think this is simply because those studies have not examined adjective subcategories in their analyses. The changes in the effects of adjective subcategories in our data are quite clear and are significant, and the development of durative/habitual *be* in a similar timeframe (something which repurposes a "spare form" to mark an aspectual distinction) may have influenced the repurposing of zero.

(3) a broader context of grammatical restructuring. The resolution to the grammatical ambiguity in AAE and to the lack of transparency within the copula/auxiliary system was triggered in part by other ongoing grammatical restructurings, in particular with developments in past habituals. The expansion of *useta* at the expense of *would be* and invariant *be* derived from *would* deletion meant that the habituality associated with *be* derived from *would* deletion could become associated with be_2 and allow it to serve as a marker of habituality in the present tense. This also meant that the shift in the function of zero from marker of verbness to marker of nonstativity did not appear de novo, but rather occurred within the broader context of the development of new aspectual markers in AAE.

(4) a sociocultural context that favored both independent linguistic developments and the spread of those developments. The Great Migration not only created vibrant new African American communities and provided an environment for the emergence of new cultural productions, it also created communication networks and an African American identity that was conducive to the spread of the kind of grammatical innovations that would help shape a distinctive African American variety.

This Element, then, documents linguistic innovation responding to grammatical ambiguities created by the inheritance of features from different sources within the context of new community formation and developing cultural identity. In doing so it demonstrates the kind of factors needed for fundamental changes in linguistic systems and for the formation of new languages more generally, and it illustrates the types of processes that were likely at work in the development of New Englishes around the world, processes that reflect the interplay of inheritance and innovation.

References

Agee, James and Walker Evans. (1941). *Let Us Now Praise Famous Men.* Cambridge, MA: The Riverside Press.

Ayers, Edward L. (1992). *The Promise of the New South: Life after Reconstruction.* New York: Oxford University Press.

Bailey, Guy. (1989). Sociolinguistic constraints on language change and the evolution of *are* in Early Modern English. In Joseph B. Trahern (ed.), *Standardizing English: Essays in the History of Language Change.* Tennessee Studies in Literature, vol. 31. Knoxville: University of Tennessee Press, 158–71.

Bailey, Guy. (1993). A perspective on African-American English. In Dennis R. Preston (ed.), *American Dialect Research.* Amsterdam: John Benjamins, 287–318.

Bailey, Guy. (1997). When did Southern American English begin? In Edgar Schneider (ed.), *Englishes around the World, Vol. 1: General – British Isles – North America. Studies in Honour of Manfred Gorlach.* Amsterdam: John Benjamins, 255–75.

Bailey, Guy. (2001). The relationship between AAVE and White vernaculars in the American South: Some phonological evidence. In Sonja Lanehart (ed.), *Sociocultural and Historical Contexts of African American English.* Amsterdam: John Benjamins, 53–92.

Bailey, Guy. (2007). Ambiguity and innovation in the evolution of African American Vernacular English. Presentation at Studies in the History of the English Language (SHEL-5). University of Georgia, Athens, Georgia.

Bailey, Guy and Marvin Bassett. (1986). Invariant *be* in the lower South. In Michael Montgomery and Guy Bailey (eds.), *Language Variety in the South: Perspectives in Black and White.* Tuscaloosa: University of Alabama Press, 158–79.

Bailey, Guy and Natalie Maynor. (1985a). The present tense of *be* in Southern Black folk speech. *American Speech* 60: 195–213.

Bailey, Guy and Natalie Maynor. (1985b). The present tense of *be* in White folk speech of the Southern United States. *English World-Wide* 6: 199–216.

Bailey, Guy and Natalie Maynor. (1987). Decreolization? *Language in Society* 16(4): 449–73.

Bailey, Guy and Natalie Maynor. (1989). The divergence controversy. *American Speech* 64: 12–39.

Bailey, Guy and Erik Thomas. (1998). Some aspects of African-American vernacular English phonology. In Salikoko S. Mufwene, John R. Rickford,

Guy Bailey, and John Baugh (eds.), *African-American English: Structure, History, and Use*. London: Routledge, 85–109.

Bailey, Guy, Natalie Maynor, and Patricia Cukor-Avila. (1989). Variation in subject-verb concord in Early Modern English. *Language Variation and Change* 1: 285–301.

Bailey, Guy, Natalie Maynor, and Patricia Cukor-Avila. (1991). *The Emergence of Black English: Texts and Commentary*. Philadelphia, PA: John Benjamins.

Bailey, Guy, Tom Wikle, Jan Tillery, and Lori Sand. (1991). The apparent time construct. *Language Variation and Change* 3: 241–64.

Bailey, Guy, Tom Wikle, Jan Tillery, and Lori Sand. (1996). The linguistic consequences of catastrophic events: An example from the American Southwest. In Jennifer Arnold, Renée Blake, Brad Davidson, Scott Schwenter, and Julie Solomon (eds.), *Sociolinguistic Variation: Data, Theory, and Analysis. Selected Papers from NWAV 23 at Stanford*. Stanford, CA: CSLI Publications, 435–51.

Baugh, Albert C. and John Cable. (2012). *A History of the English Language*, 6th ed. New York: Routledge.

Baugh, John. (1980). A re-examination of the Black English copula. In William Labov (ed.), *Locating Language in Time and Space*. New York: Academic Press, 83–106.

Bickerton, Derek. (1981). *Roots of Language*. Ann Arbor, MI: Karoma Press.

Blake, Renée. (1997). Defining the envelope of linguistic variation: The case of "don't count" forms in the copula analysis of African American English. *Language Variation and Change* 9: 57–79.

Buschfeld, Sarah, Thomas Hoffmann, Magnus Huber, and Alexander Kautzsch. (2014). The dynamic model and beyond. In Sarah Buschfeld, Thomas Hoffmann, Magnus Huber, and Alexander Kautzsch (eds.), *The Evolution of Englishes: The Dynamic Model and Beyond*. Amsterdam: John Benjamins, 1–17.

Comrie, Bernard. (1976). *Aspect*. Cambridge: Cambridge University Press.

Cukor-Avila, Patricia. (1995). The evolution of AAVE in a rural community: An ethnolinguistic study. Unpublished Ph.D. thesis, University of Michigan.

Cukor-Avila, Patricia. (1999). Stativity and copula absence in AAVE: Grammatical constraints at the subcategorical level. *Journal of English Linguistics* 27: 341–55.

Cukor-Avila, Patricia. (2001). Co-existing grammars: The relationship between the evolution of AAVE and WVE in the South. In Sonja Lanehart (ed.), *Sociocultural and Historical Contexts of African American English*. Amsterdam: John Benjamins, 93–127.

Cukor-Avila, Patricia. (2002). *She say, she go, she be like*: Verbs of quotation over time in African American Vernacular English. *American Speech* 77(1): 3–31.

Cukor-Avila, Patricia. (2012). Some structural consequences of diffusion. *Language in Society* 41: 1–26.

Cukor-Avila, Patricia and Guy Bailey. (1995a). An approach to sociolinguistic fieldwork. *English World-Wide* 16: 159–93.

Cukor-Avila, Patricia and Guy Bailey. (1995b). Grammaticalization in AAVE. In Jocelyn Ayers, Leela Bilmes, Joshua S. Guenter, Barbara A. Kaiser, and Ju Namkung (eds.), *Proceedings of the Twenty-First Annual Meeting of the Berkeley Linguistics Society*. Berkeley, CA: Berkeley Linguistics Society, 401–13.

Cukor-Avila, Patricia and Guy Bailey. (2001). The effects of the race of the interviewer on sociolinguistic fieldwork. *Journal of Sociolinguistics* 5(2): 254–70.

Cukor-Avila, Patricia and Guy Bailey. (2007). Age-grading and linguistic diffusion. Plenary at New Ways of Analyzing Variation (NWAV-36). University of Pennsylvania.

Cukor-Avila, Patricia and Guy Bailey. (2011). The interaction of transition and diffusion in the spread of linguistic forms. *University of Pennsylvania Working Papers in Linguistics* 17(2): 41–49.

Cukor-Avila, Patricia and Guy Bailey. (2013). Real and apparent time. In J. K. Chambers and Natalie Schilling (eds.), *The Handbook of Language Variation and Change*, 2nd ed. New York: John Wiley & Sons, 239–62.

Cukor-Avila, Patricia and Guy Bailey. (2015). Rural Texas African American Vernacular English. In Sonja Lanehart (ed.), *The Oxford Handbook of African American Language*. Oxford: Oxford University Press, 181–200.

Cukor-Avila, Patricia and Guy Bailey. (2017). The effect of small *N*s and gaps in contact on panel survey data. In Suzanne E. Wagner and Isa Buchstaller (eds.), *Panel Studies of Variation and Change*. New York: Routledge, 181–212.

D'Arcy, Alexandra. (2021). Reconfiguring quotation over time and the system-internal rise of BE *like*. In Peter J. Grund and Terry Walker (eds.), *Speech Representation in the History of English*. Oxford: Oxford University Press, 73–101.

Dayton, Elizabeth. (1996). Grammatical categories of the verb in African-American Vernacular English. Unpublished Ph.D. thesis, University of Pennsylvania.

Du Wes, Giles. (1972 facsimile reprint of 1532 edition). *An Introduction for to Learn to Read, to Pronounce, and to Speak French*. Menston, England: The Scholar Press.

Ewers, Traute. (1996). *The Origin of American Black English: Be-Forms in the HOODOO Texts*. Berlin: Mouton.

Fasold, Ralph. (1972). *Tense Marking in Black English: A Linguistic and Social Analysis*. Washington, DC: Center for Applied Linguistics.

Fisher, Sabriya. (2018). Change over time in the grammar of African American English. University of Pennsylvania Working Papers in Linguistics: Selected Papers from New Ways of Analyzing Variation (NWAV46) 24(2): 29–38.

Freedman, David A. (2009). *Statistical Models: Theory and Practice*. Cambridge: Cambridge University Press.

Fruehwald, Josef. (2017). Generations, lifespans, and the zeitgeist. *Language Variation and Change* 29: 1–27.

Green, Lisa. (1998). Aspect and predicate phrases in African-American vernacular English. In Salikoko S. Mufwene, John R. Rickford, Guy Bailey, and John Baugh (eds.), *African-American English: Structure, History, and Use*. London: Routledge, 37–68.

Green, Lisa. (2011). *Language and the African American Child*. Cambridge: Cambridge University Press.

Gregory, James N. (2006). *The Southern Diaspora: How the Great Migration of Black and White Southerners Transformed America*. Chapel Hill: University of North Carolina Press.

Groh, George W. (1972). *The Black Migration: The Journey to Urban America*. New York: Weybright and Talley.

Hamilton, C. Horace. (1972). The Negro leaves the South. In Helen MacGill Hughes (ed.), *Population Growth and the Complex Society*. Boston, MA: Allyn and Bacon, 79–90.

Harrison, James A. (1884). Negro English. *Anglia* 7: 232–79.

Hengeveld, Kees. (2011). The grammaticalization of tense and aspect. In Bernd Heine and Heiko Narrog (eds.), *The Oxford Handbook of Grammaticalization*. Oxford: Oxford University Press, 581–94.

Hockett, Charles. (1958). *A Course in Modern Linguistics*. New York: Macmillan.

Holm, John. (1984). Variability of the copula in Black English and its creole kin. *American Speech* 59: 291–309.

Holm, John. (1988). *Pidgins and Creoles*, vol. 1. Cambridge: Cambridge University Press.

Holm, John. (2004). *Languages in Contact: The Partial Restructuring of Vernaculars*. Cambridge: Cambridge University Press.

Jones, Marcus E. (1980). *Black Migration in the United States with Emphasis on Selected Central Cities*. Saratoga, CA: Century Twenty One.

Kautzsch, Alexander. (2002). *The Historical Evolution of Earlier African American English*. Berlin: Mouton de Gruyter.

Kautzsch, Alexander. (2012). Earlier African American English. In Bernd Kortmann and Kerstin Lunkenheimer (eds.), *The Mouton World Atlas of Variation in English*. Berlin: Mouton de Gruyter, 126–40.

Kendall, Tyler and Charlie Farrington. (2021). *The Corpus of Regional African American Language, Version 2021.07*. Eugene, OR: The Online Resources for African American Language Project, https://oraal.uoregon.edu/coraal.

La Mayre, Marten. (1977 facsimile reprint of 1606 edition). *The Dutch School-Master*. Menston, England: The Scholar Press.

Labov, William. (1963). The social motivation of a sound change. *Word* 19: 273–309.

Labov, William. (1966). *The Social Stratification of English in New York City*. Washington, DC: Center for Applied Linguistics.

Labov, William. (1969). Contraction, deletion, and inherent variability of the English copula. *Language* 45: 715–762.

Labov, William. (1972a). *Sociolinguistic Patterns*. Philadelphia: University of Pennsylvania Press.

Labov, William. (1972b). *Language in the Inner City*. Philadelphia: University of Pennsylvania Press.

Labov, William. (1994). *Principles of Linguistic Change, Vol. I: Internal Factors*. Cambridge: Cambridge University Press.

Labov, William. (2001). *Principles of Linguistic Change, Vol. II: Social Factors*. Cambridge: Cambridge University Press.

Labov, William. (2007). Transmission and diffusion. *Language* 83(2): 344–87.

Labov, William. (2010). *Principles of Linguistic Change, Vol. III: Cognitive and Cultural Factors*. Cambridge: Cambridge University Press.

Labov, William, Paul Cohen, Clarence Robbins, and John Lewis. (1968). *A Study of the Non-Standard English of Negro and Puerto Rican Speakers in New York City*, 2 vols. Philadelphia, PA: US Regional Survey.

Lanehart, Sonja. (ed.). (2015). *The Oxford Handbook of African American Language*. Oxford: Oxford University Press.

Langacker, Ronald W. (1977). Syntactic Reanalysis. In Charles N. Li (ed.), *Mechanisms of Syntactic Change*. Austin: University of Texas Press, 57–139.

Lehmann, Nicholas. (1992). *The Promised Land: The Great Black Migration and How It Changed America*. New York: Knopf.

McWhorter, John H. (1998). Identifying the creole prototype: Vindicating a typological class. *Language* 74(4): 788–818.

Miethaner, Ulrich. (2014). Innovation in pre-World War II African American Vernacular English? Evidence from BLUR. In Sarah Buschfeld,

Thomas Hoffmann, Magnus Huber, and Alexander Kautzsch (eds.), *The Evolution of Englishes*, Varieties of English Around the World G49. Amsterdam: John Benjamins, 365–85.

Moore, Samuel and Albert H. Marckwardt. (1969). *Historical Outlines of English Sounds and Inflections*. Berlin: George H. Wahr.

Mufwene, Salikoko S. (1996a). Creole genesis: A population genetics perspective. In Pauline Christie (ed.), *Caribbean Language Issues Old and New*. Kingston, Jamaica: University Press of the West Indies, 163–96.

Mufwene, Salikoko S. (1996b). The Founder Principle in creole genesis. *Diachronica* 13: 83–134.

Mufwene, Salikoko S. (2015). The emergence of African American English: Monogenetic or polygenetic? With or without "decreolization?" Under how much substrate influence? In Sonja Lanehart (ed.), *The Oxford Handbook of African American Language*. Oxford: Oxford University Press, 57–84.

Pederson, Lee, Guy H. Bailey, Marvin W. Bassett, Charles E. Billiard, and Susan E. Leas. (1981). *Linguistic Atlas of the Gulf States: The Basic Materials*. Ann Arbor, MI: University Microfilms.

Pérez, José Ramón Varela. (2013). Operator and negative contraction in spoken British English: A change in progress. In Bas Aarts, Joanne Close, Geoffrey Leech, and Sean Wallis (eds.), *The Verb Phrase in English: Investigating Recent Language Change with Corpora*. Cambridge: Cambridge University Press, 256–85.

Poplack, Shana. (ed.). (2000). *The English History of African American English*. Malden, MA: Blackwell.

Poplack, Shana and David Sankoff. (1987). The Philadelphia story in the Spanish Caribbean. *American Speech* 62: 291–314.

Poplack, Shana and Sali Tagliamonte. (2001). *African American English in the Diaspora*. Malden, MA: Blackwell.

Rickford, John R. (1986). Some principles for the study of Black and White speech in the South. In Michael B. Montgomery and Guy Bailey (eds.), *Language Variety in the South*. Tuscaloosa: University of Alabama Press, 38–62.

Rickford, John R. (1992). Grammatical variation and divergence. In Marinel Gerristen and Dieter Stein (eds.), *Internal and External Factors in Language Change*. The Hague: Mouton, 175–200.

Rickford, John R. (1998). The creole origins of African-American Vernacular English: Evidence from copula absence. In Salikoko S. Mufwene, John R. Rickford, Guy Bailey, and John Baugh (eds.), *African-American English: Structure, History, and Use*. London: Routledge, 154–200.

Rickford, John R. (2006). Down for the count: The creole origins hypothesis of AAVE at the hands of the Ottawa circle, and their supporters. *Journal of Pidgin and Creole Languages* 21(1): 97–155.

Rickford, John. R. (2015). The creole origins hypothesis. In Sonja Lanehart (ed.), *The Oxford Handbook of African American Language*. Oxford: Oxford University Press, 35–56.

Rickford, John R. and Mackenzie Price (2013). Girlz to women: Age-grading, language change, and stylistic variation. *Journal of Sociolinguistics* 17: 143–79.

Rickford, John R., Arnetha Ball, Renée Blake, Raina Jackson, and Nomi Martin. (1992). Rappin' on the copula coffin: Theoretical and methodological issues in the analysis of copula variation in African-American Vernacular English. *Language Variation and Change* 3: 103–32.

Romaine, Suzanne. (1982). *Socio-Historical Linguistics: Its Status and Methodology*. Cambridge: Cambridge University Press.

Romaine, Suzanne. (1988). *Pidgin and Creole Languages*. London: Routledge.

Sankoff, Gillian. (2005). Cross-sectional and longitudinal studies in sociolinguistics. In Ulrich Ammon, Norbert Dittmar, Klaus J. Mattheier, and Peter Trudgill (eds.), *International Handbook of the Science of Language and Society*, vol. 2. Berlin: Mouton de Gruyter, 1003–13.

Sankoff, Gillian. (2018). Language change across the lifespan. *The Annual Review of Linguistics* 4: 297–316.

Sankoff, Gillian and Hélene Blondeau. (2007). Language change across the lifespan: /r/ in Montreal French. *Language* 83: 560–88.

Schneider, Edgar W. (1989). *American Earlier Black English*. Tuscaloosa: University of Alabama Press.

Schneider, Edgar W. (2003). The dynamics of New Englishes: From identity construction to dialect birth. *Language* 79(2): 233–81.

Schneider, Edgar W. (2007). *Postcolonial English: Varieties Around the World*. Cambridge: Cambridge University Press.

Schneider, Edgar. (2015). Documenting the history of African American Vernacular English: A survey and assessment of sources and results. In Sonja Lanehart (ed.), *The Oxford Handbook of African American Language*. Oxford: Oxford University Press, 125–39.

Smith, K. Aaron. (2018). A usage-based account for the historical reflexes of *ain't* in AAE. In K. Aaron Smith and Dawn Nordquist (eds.), *Functionalist and Usage-Based Approaches to the Study of Language in Honor of Joan I. Bybee*. Amsterdam: John Benjamins, 155–73.

Smith, T. Lynn. (1966). The redistribution of the Negro population of the United States, 1910–1960. *Journal of Negro History* 51: 155–73.

Spears, Arthur. (2008). Pidgins, creoles, and African American English. In Silvia Kouwenberg and John Victor Singler (eds.), *The Handbook of Pidgins and Creoles*. Malden, MA: Blackwell, 512–42.

Stewart, William A. (1967). Sociolinguistic factors in the history of American Negro dialects. *The Florida FL Reporter* 5(2): 11, 22, 24, 26.

Stewart, William A. (1968). Continuity and change in American Negro dialects. *The Florida FL Reporter* 62: 14–16, 18, 304.

Tagliamonte, Sali A. (2013). *Roots of English: Exploring the History of Dialects*. Cambridge: Cambridge University Press.

Tagliamonte, Sali A. and Alexandra D'Arcy. (2009). Peaks beyond phonology: Adolescence, incrementation, and language change. *Language* 85(1): 58–108.

Tagliamonte, Sali A., Alexandra D'Arcy, and Celeste Rodríguez Louro. (2016). Outliers, impact, and rationalization in linguistic change. *Language* 92(4): 301–26.

Tagliamonte, Sali A., Mercedes Durham, and Jennifer Smith. (2014). Grammaticalization at an early stage: Future *be going to* in conservative British dialects. *English Language and Linguistics* 18(1): 75–108.

Thomas, Erik and Guy Bailey. (1998). Parallels between vowel subsystems of African American Vernacular English and Caribbean Anglophone Creoles. *Journal of Pidgin and Creole Languages* 13: 267–96.

Thomas, William. (1968 facsimile reprint of 1550 edition). *Principal Rules of the Italian Grammar*. Menston, England: The Scholar Press.

Tillery, Jan and Guy Bailey. (2003). Urbanization and the evolution of Southern American English. In Steven J. Nagle and Sara L. Sanders (eds.), *English in the Southern United States*. Cambridge: Cambridge University Press, 159–72.

Tillery, Jan, Guy Bailey, and Tom Wikle. (2004). Demographic change and American dialectology in the twenty-first century. *American Speech* 79(3): 227–49.

Van Herk, Gerard. (2015). The English origins hypothesis. In Sonja Lanehart (ed.), *The Oxford Handbook of African American Language*. Oxford: Oxford University Press, 23–34.

Wagner, Suzanne E. (2012). Age-grading in sociolinguistic theory. *Language and Linguistics Compass* 6: 371–82.

Weinreich, Uriel, William Labov, and Marvin I. Herzog. (1968). Empirical foundations for a theory of language change. In Winfred P. Lehmann and Yakov Malkiel (eds.), *Directions for Historical Linguistics*. Austin: University of Texas Press, 95–188.

Weldon, Tracy. (2003). Revisiting the creolist hypothesis: Copula variability in Gullah and Southern rural AAVE. *American Speech* 78: 171–191.

Wilkerson, Isabel. (2010). *The Warmth of Other Suns: The Epic Story of America's Great Migration*. New York: Random House.

Winford, Donald. (1997). On the origins of African American Vernacular English: A creolist perspective. Part 1: The sociohistorical background. *Diachronica* 19: 305–44.

Winford, Donald. (1998). On the origins of African American Vernacular English – A creolist perspective. Part II: Linguistic features. *Diachronica* 20: 99–154.

Winford, Donald. (2015). The origins of African American Vernacular English: Beginnings. In Sonja Lanehart (ed.), *The Oxford Handbook of African American Language*. Oxford: Oxford University Press, 85–104.

Wolfram, Walter A. (1969). *A Sociolinguistic Description of Detroit Negro Speech*. Washington, DC: Center for Applied Linguistics.

Wolfram, Walt. (1974). The relationship of white Southern speech to vernacular Black English. *Language* 50: 498–527.

Wolfram, Walt and Erik Thomas. (2008). *The Development of African American English*. Oxford: Wiley-Blackwell.

Cambridge Elements ☰

World Englishes

Edgar W. Schneider
University of Regensburg

Edgar W. Schneider is Professor Emeritus of English Linguistics at the University of Regensburg, Germany. His many books include *Postcolonial English* (Cambridge, 2007), *English around the World, 2e* (Cambridge, 2020) and *The Cambridge Handbook of World Englishes* (Cambridge, 2020).

About the Series
Over the last centuries, the English language has spread all over the globe due to a multitude of factors including colonization and globalization. In investigating these phenomena, the vibrant linguistic sub-discipline of "World Englishes" has grown substantially, developing appropriate theoretical frameworks and considering applied issues. This Elements series will cover all the topics of the discipline in an accessible fashion and will be supplemented by on-line material.

Cambridge Elements ≡

World Englishes

Lightning Source UK Ltd.
Milton Keynes UK
UKHW020655171022
410608UK00018B/1022